CAN
ETHICS
BE
TAUGHT?

CAN ETHICS BE TAUGHT?

*Perspectives, Challenges, and Approaches
at Harvard Business School*

THOMAS R. PIPER

MARY C. GENTILE

SHARON DALOZ PARKS

Foreword by John H. McArthur

HARVARD BUSINESS SCHOOL
BOSTON, MASSACHUSETTS

97 96 95 94 93   5 4 3 2 1

Piper, Thomas R.
Can ethics be taught? : perspectives, challenges, and
approaches
at the Harvard Business School / Thomas R. Piper, Mary C.
Gentile, and Sharon Daloz Parks.
p.   cm.
Includes bibliographical references and index.
ISBN 0-87584-400-6 (alk. paper)
1. Business ethics—Study and teaching (Graduate)—United
States. 2. Business education—United States. 3. Master of
business administration degree—United States. 4. Harvard
University. Graduate School of Business Administration—
Curricula. I. Gentile. Mary C. II. Parks. Sharon Daloz. III.
Title.
HF5387.P56   1993
174'.4'071173—dc20   92-27077
                                                          CIP

The paper used in this publication meets the requirements of
the American National Standard for Permanence of Paper
for Printed Library Materials Z.39.48-1984.

To John Matthews

*In memory and appreciation of a life's commitment
to the conviction that ethical values can and must be
central to the education of managers and business leaders.*

Contents

Foreword

This book, which represents the work of Thomas R. Piper and his colleagues in Harvard Business School's Program in Leadership, Ethics, and Corporate Responsibility, is a remarkable achievement. It documents the results of five years of risk-taking, persistence, and productivity.

But I think this book, and the work it comprises, are even more remarkable when they are considered in their context. Let me recreate that context.

In March 1987, I had the opportunity to speak to the Harvard Business School Club of Greater New York. I used that occasion to announce a major gift to the school by John S. R. Shad, a distinguished graduate of the school. Mr. Shad's gift was to be used to support school-based initiatives in ethics and leadership. These initiatives, although still to be defined, were expected to include research, curriculum and faculty development, recognition awards, and publications—on a scale that had never before been attempted, either at our school or elsewhere.

As the reader will recall, this was a period of intense national interest in ethical issues. At that time, it seemed as if each morning's paper brought us unwelcome news of yet another leader who was morally bankrupt. Failed leaders were being revealed in every walk of life: business, government, religion, medicine, law, and so on. These sad examples of excess, greed, and cynicism were among the factors that helped prompt John Shad to make his magnificent gift to the school. Serving then as an outstanding and activist chairman of the Securities and Exchange Commission, Mr. Shad was profoundly disappointed at how frequently the graduates of some of our finest business and law schools were involved, in one way or another, in the cases then being brought before the SEC. Surely, this very principled man felt, we could do better. Surely the school had a bigger responsibility and a role to play in all of this. This was his challenge to us.

Concurrently, and closer to home, leaders at Harvard were also attempting to grapple with these troubling issues. Principal among them was Derek Bok, then president of this university, who was appropriately relentless in his efforts to focus our professional schools on the challenges of personal and group responsibility. This was not only a societal need, he argued with passion, but an urgent need of the academy: learning and discovery simply could not take place in an ethical vacuum, without the mooring of moral standards. Nor, he argued further, could professionals from our graduate schools practice in a moral and ethical void. By habit, example, and exhortation, he helped articulate those standards and expectations for all of us.

On the morning after my speech in New York, Tom Piper came to see me. He told me that he felt very strongly about the program initiative implicit in the gift I had just announced, and that he would very much like to play a leading role in the new effort. From my perspective, that was extraordinarily good news. As Senior Associate Dean for Educational Programs, Tom was known among the faculty as the individual who somehow juggled our limited bodies to staff all our teaching and research programs appropriately, while providing his colleagues with ample opportunities for personal experimentation and growth. No other person among us has been able to accomplish so many of these things with his colleagues as has Tom during my years at the school. If anyone could break molds, reconfigure the landscape, and perhaps build a new kind of ethical emphasis into the fabric of our school, it was Tom. I knew this. I was encouraged and immeasurably grateful for his interest in this difficult new venture.

Samuel Butler once observed that "we are not won by arguments that we can analyze, but by tone and temper, by the manner which is the man himself." An effort such as this would need someone blessed with Tom's manner, and endowed with his rare degree of clarity and conscience and energy if it was to prosper.

Truth be told, I'm not sure Tom knew exactly what he was getting into when he volunteered to lead this effort, which eventually became known as the Program in Leadership, Ethics, and Corporate Responsibility. The school's various experiments in ethical training in the past are explained elsewhere in this volume, and I won't recapitulate them here. Suffice it to say that we already had behind us several decades of experience in the field. These decades were dominated by two recurring themes. First, we tended to alternate between "stand-alone" ethics courses, on the one hand, and ethics-related teaching that was more or less integrated into the standard curriculum. (At this institution, such a pattern of alternation generally means that no single approach is proving satisfactory.) Second, we had numerous examples of quite remarkable and deeply committed individuals among us who felt a strong personal commitment to the field, and who advanced it up to a point, but who ultimately found themselves unable to scale up their activities into a large and durable effort. As a result, few of those who tried truly changed the nature of the educational process at the school. At no point in our history, until now, did we ever break through in this domain of ethical training such that a broad group of faculty and students wanted to join in a committed, sustained fashion. "Desire outruns performance," as one of my predecessors once concluded bleakly, "all along the line."

In the past five years, Tom and his colleagues have broken out of both of these traps. They have aimed, explicitly and successfully, at both the warp and woof of our curriculum. Yes, they have designed a highly effective free-standing ethics module for the first year of the MBA program; but they also worked with the first-year course heads in order to promote a true integration of value-based decision making *throughout* the curriculum. They have examined every other aspect of our MBA experience, as well—including admissions, the acculturation process, and extracurricular activities—to determine what signals we can and should send to our students. Where our knowledge has proved to be incomplete, they have undertaken the extremely difficult process of coining new intellectual capital. Where our tools have proved to be inadequate, they have helped invent new ones. In addition, and in part to counter the charge that we should *practice* what we preach, others, led by Earl Sasser and Jim Cash, have helped bring into being a vast program of community service activities, involving several hundred students and employees of the school annually in activities here in Boston and around the globe. For the first time in our history, we have a strong group of young colleagues coming along in this important, challenging domain, including Joe Badaracco, Greg Dees, and Lynn Paine. Through all of these efforts, I believe that those involved have held up a new mirror to our community. All of these things taken as a whole are truly changing an important dimension of the learning process at this school.

This book is a piece of that composite mirror. Sharon Daloz Parks's work, described in Chapter Two, tells us more than we have ever known about the values, priorities, hopes, and receptiveness of our MBA students. Mary C. Gentile's work and careful documentation of faculty reactions and contributions to the Leadership, Ethics, and Corporate Responsibility initiative, as described in Chapter Three, should serve future faculty leaders well as they undertake initiatives of similar scope and consequence. Change, especially planned change, is never easy. We should take note when it is done with care and grace.

But again, this book is only one manifestation of a highly

significant venture. As I fully expected, Tom Piper and his colleagues created a small juggernaut. They launched an entrepreneurial venture that now possesses great momentum. They brought in new people, and (much more difficult!) they found ways to involve, motivate, and reorient our existing personnel. Taking a broader view, they provided a map that other professional schools should find extremely useful. In our conversations and in his writing, Tom emphasized the critical importance of the "schools of life"—those corporations and institutions that hire our graduates, and which must take responsibility for helping those young people connect principle and purpose to their professional lives. For these organizations, too, this book has great relevance.

As Tom says in his concluding chapter, it is far too early to declare this initiative an unqualified success. I suggest that we wait twenty years, look around us, and then make that important assessment. Meanwhile, let's celebrate the fact that the pot is now beginning to boil. The program has attracted remarkable leadership so far, and under its auspices, many colleagues are finally working together at this school to respond to the challenge posed to us by John Shad. An extremely significant enterprise is well under way.

John H. McArthur, Dean
Harvard Business School
Boston, Massachusetts
November 1992

Acknowledgments

It takes a wide network of collegial commitment to readdress ethics in the contemporary business curriculum. This work represents the investment of a great number of people who made vital contributions to the work this volume describes and to the volume itself. We acknowledge with respect and deep gratitude that these people were themselves encouraged, inspired, and mentored by a host of others whose lives across generations are indirectly but just as surely a part of this work.

We want to specifically recognize and express our appreciation to a few key individuals at Harvard Business School who held the "ethics conversation" with commitment and competence over decades past and whose work served as a sturdy root system, nurturing and informing the present effort. They are John B. Matthews, who taught Business Ethics at Harvard Business School for three decades and to whom this volume is dedicated, and Kenneth A. Andrews. Both of these individuals, by the content of their teaching, publishing, and the demonstrated quality of their personal and public values, forged important pathways toward the effort that is in place today. In the initial phase of the present work, Kenneth E. Goodpaster played an important role in the teaching and development of a new ethics curriculum. There also are a number of alumni and donors who have expressed their concern, vision, and commitment with strategic generosity.

Institutional leadership was critical to the success of this effort, and we are grateful to Derek Bok, president of Harvard University during the formative period of this initiative, John McArthur, dean of the school, and Dennis Thompson, professor and director, Harvard University Program in Ethics and the Professions.

The principal colleagues in the development of the ethics curriculum and particularly in the development of the module in Decision Making and Ethical Values were those who during these first five years served in the teaching group for the module with courage, imagination, and personal commitment: James Austin, Joseph Badaracco, Michael Beer, Thomas Bonoma, Raymond Corey, Dwight Crane, Gregory Dees, Robert Hayes, Kenneth Goodpaster, George Lodge, John Matthews, Cynthia Montgomery, Lynn Sharp Paine, Earl Sasser, Howard Stevenson, and Shoshana Zuboff. Their efforts were enabled by the dedicated research and program development of Audrey Sullivan Jacobs and Kimerer LaMothe who in the formative stages gave substance and shape to the emerging program.

Other colleagues who served in notably substantial ways to encourage the wider effort to incorporate ethics across the functional areas, in both the first- and second-year courses as well as the wider life of the school are Henry B. Arthur, Louis Barnes, Mary Barth, William Bruns, James Cash, John Gabarro, Julie Hertenstein, Rosabeth Kanter, Laura Nash, John Quelch, Kasturi Rangan, Roy Shapiro, Craig Smith, John Sviokla, Richard Tedlow, Barbara Toffler, David Upton, and Steven Wheelwright. This list is much too short if we also consider the many other faculty who through their teaching and openness created broad support for this effort throughout Harvard Business School. The program itself has been enriched through the leadership of Earl Sasser, who when faculty chair of the MBA Program, fostered the development of projects that allowed members of the school to give their energy and extend their learning through involvement in the Boston-Cambridge community.

In support of the research in Chapter Two, Karen Thorkilsen, research associate, played a critical role, bringing to the work not only competent research skills but also an informed commitment, which helped refine and enhance the research process. The colleagueship with Darden and Tuck as represented by researchers Rosalyn Berne and Deborah Chapman has brought both scope and depth to our conviction that the issues addressed here are important across a wider population. Eugenie Moriconi and Kate Marrone contributed both transcription skills and a committed understanding, which enriched the project.

Many colleagues read and helpfully commented on all or portions of the manuscript. We are, therefore, indebted to Kenneth Andrews, Joseph Badaracco, Patricia K. Light, Laurent A. Parks Daloz, Meryl Reis Leous, George Lodge, Warren McFarlan, William G. Perry, George Rupp, and Earl Sasser. We have also benefited from the assistance of three editors: Jeffrey Cruikshank, Natalie Greenberg, and John Simon. Patrick Amory, Rita Colella, Eugenie Moriconi, Paula Puhak, and Bill Whelan graciously assisted in the production and reproduction of numerous drafts.

Finally, we are grateful to the many faculty and students who generously agreed to be interviewed on behalf of this effort to better understand how the business curriculum may be most usefully and strategically responsive to the challenges facing business managers, both now and into a rapidly changing future. We promised them anonymity but our gratitude must be public.

CAN
ETHICS
BE
TAUGHT?

CHAPTER ONE

Rediscovery of Purpose: The Genesis of the Leadership, Ethics, and Corporate Responsibility Initiative

THOMAS R. PIPER

> What is most important is that management realize that it must consider the impact of every business policy and business action upon society. It has to consider whether the action is likely to promote the public good, to advance the basic beliefs of our society, to contribute to its stability, strength, and harmony.
>
> Peter Drucker, *The Practice of Management* 1955, p. 342

> The success of management . . . has greatly changed management's *meaning*. Its success has made management the general, the pervasive function, and the distinct organization of our society of organizations. As such, management inevitably has become "affected with the public interest." To work out what this means for management theory and management practice will constitute the "management problems" of the next fifty years.
>
> Peter Drucker, *The Frontiers of Management* 1986, pp. 192–193

A strong sense of leadership, ethics, and responsibility is asked of business today if it is to meet the expectations and urgent requirements of society. The United States is confronted by an array of issues that challenge its well-being; among them are issues related to the environment, industrial competitiveness, the educational system, the decay of inner cities, the assimilation of a diverse work force, and the balancing of work and family. Progress will be made only if business institutions and leaders are active partners in the solutions.

Yet the very businesses and business people expected to provide answers and solutions are suffering from diminished trust and increasing challenges to their legitimacy. Disaffection toward the workplace has increased, while employee mistrust, doubt, and resentment of senior management have deepened.

1

Workers' willingness to embrace new technologies, to take risks, and to commit to new standards of productivity and quality has been eroded by distrust.[1]

Employee cynicism is accompanied by an even broader societal cynicism about our political and economic systems and, more specifically, about business. When the Gallup organization surveyed American public opinion in 1988 to discover in which institutions people had the most confidence, big business ranked last in a list of ten. Only twenty-five percent of those asked had "a great deal or quite a lot of confidence in it," down from thirty-two percent in 1979, when it also appeared last on the list.[2] The trend has been in evidence for a number of years. In 1968, Yankelovich and Skelly reported that seventy percent of the American people believed that business tried to strike a balance between profits and the public interest; only fifteen percent believed so ten years later.[3] And whereas a 1971 Harris poll found that twenty-seven percent of those surveyed had "a great deal of confidence in the people running major companies," a 1991 poll revealed that the figure had dropped to fifteen percent.[4]

Kanter and Mirvis conclude from a national survey in the late 1980s that "Cynical tendencies are growing into a consensus world view with implications for society, commerce, and the workplace. Some forty-three percent of the American populace fit the profile of the cynic, who sees selfishness and fakery at the core of human nature. . . . Cynics mistrust politicians and most authority figures, regard the average person as false-faced and uncaring, and conclude that you should basically look out for yourself. . . . Cynics at work deeply doubt the truth of what their managements tell them and believe that their companies, given a chance, will take advantage of them."[5]

These perceptions, even if exaggerated, profoundly affect managers' authority—their ability to lead and to meet the challenges and opportunities of their positions. Furthermore, these perceptions will shape a regulatory environment that itself may be destructive in societal terms. Our society cannot function effectively, cannot resolve the issues that challenge it, in the face of pervasive cynicism. Outstanding organizations cannot be created in a sea of distrust.

It is in this context of flux and challenge and failing faith that business educators must somehow prepare their students to assume roles of social and fiduciary responsibility. Business and government most often fail to meet their responsibilities not from an inadequacy of tools, techniques, and theory but from an absence of vision, a failure of leadership, an inconsistency or insufficiency of values that saps all sense of individual or organizational purpose and responsibility. It is this concern—involving our individual and organizational sense of purpose and set of principles—that management education must address. Cynicism must be replaced by a sense of purpose, worth, responsibility and accountability, and hope.

Ironically, as the corporation's role is increasingly recognized to be more complex than that of a profit-maximizing agent for its shareholders, consideration of professional ideals has given way in the MBA curriculum to emphasis on quantification, formal models, and formulas, all of which minimize the application of judgment and the debate about values.[6] Authority has retreated to that which is known, certain, and demonstrable. The issues of leadership, ethics, and corporate responsibility, in their precarious journey from "is" to "ought" to "can be,"[7] in their search for purpose that will tap the soul and energize individuals and organizations alike, call for imagination and reflection. They call for the taking of a circuitous route complete with complexity, judgment, and the explicit, painful recognition of the human consequences of management action. It is little wonder that this enterprise is too often neglected by a generation excited by the prospect of attaining the status of science, eager for analytics that will provide clear answers, and uncomfortable with ambiguity and the discussion of values.

Is it the responsibility of management education to address

these issues? Some would say no, that the requisite faculty training is absent; that ethics represents yet another subject in curricula already overcrowded; that the values of management students are already fully formed and not amenable to review or revision in the classroom.

These arguments, while useful in portraying the challenges, seem unconvincing in their conclusion. Surely business education must be an enterprise of both the intellect and the spirit—an endeavor that engages one's character and values, spurs one's imagination and sense of meaning, and stimulates one's sense of responsibility and accountability and one's desire to lead and create. Pragmatism and professionalism need to be "attached to a purpose, and that purpose to other people in some substantial way, and to larger purposes."[8]

The accomplishments of management education over the past thirty years are significant. The extraordinary growth of theory and analytics has contributed importantly to managerial competence and gained respectability for business schools within the university. But management education can and should be more than the transfer of skills and knowledge; it should be a moral endeavor, a passing-on from one generation to the next of a kind of wisdom about what is worthy of one's commitment. Faculty at professional schools have an opportunity to help students connect their capacity for high achievement to a sense of purpose, to forge a connection between self and social issues, between self and social fabric.

This joining of career to purpose and principle is in part to provide graduates with a sense of excitement and worth for their professional lives as business leaders. Not to do so would be a tragedy and a fundamental failure of education. The popularity of MBA programs—beneficiaries in recent years of soaring numbers of applications from outstanding men and women—can be cited as empirical evidence of the attraction to careers in business. These numbers say nothing, though, about the commitment of these individuals or about the reasons for their choice.

But the joining of career and purpose is necessary also to ensure both a full understanding of the responsibilities that their future positions of power will entail and a thorough sense of accountability for the results of their stewardship. The exercise of basic managerial skills in an atmosphere of uncritical moral and social premises leads not only to the proliferation of external regulation and adversarialism, but also to the widespread and justifiable lack of trust that diminishes the effectiveness of individuals and organizations.

In *One L,* Scott Turow quotes from the opening lecture of one of his law professors:

> "You are going to have an enormous power to do bad things when you finish your education here. When you get into practice, you'll be shocked at the incredible opportunities you have to mess up other people's lives. That's not funny," he told us, "although for some reason most law school professors don't like to talk about the destructive capacity you'll all hold as lawyers. I hope we can talk about that in here, and I also hope we can talk about some of the good things you can do, which, unfortunately, are often a little harder to accomplish."[9]

Some would argue that it is too late to raise questions of values and corporate purpose with students who are in their twenties and thirties, that such students are totally formed and unchangeable. We reject this assertion emphatically. These students are at a critical stage in the development of their perceptions about capitalism, business practice, leadership, and the appropriate resolution of ethical dilemmas in business (see Chapter Two). This is a period for inquiry and reflection; extended time is necessary to develop sufficient strength and sophistication to acknowledge the presence of ethical dilemmas, to imagine what could be, to recognize explicitly avoidable and unavoidable harms. It takes time to develop tough-minded individuals with the courage to act—especially when it is so much easier to take refuge in the psychological safety of distant analytics, and of remote but comforting rationalization. As John Akers, chairman of IBM, observed:

> An enormous amount of work needs to be done to get young people to think straight about questions like these [South African divestiture, production of weapons for the Pentagon, setting up of a day care center], which defy facile pseudo-moralistic answers; which require incisive definition and analysis; a clearheaded understanding of a company's sometimes conflicting responsibilities—to its stockholders, employees, and country—responsibilities that often come down to some agonizingly difficult trade-offs.[10]

Management educators also need to recognize that they have always taught lessons in leadership, ethics, and corporate responsibility, even (perhaps especially) when they are silent. Efforts as faculty to remain in a zone of value-neutrality fail. Students arrive at professional schools wondering what is valued, what is rewarded, what has legitimacy and authority. As Harvard psychiatrist Robert Coles has pointed out, what faculty are silent about and what they omit send a powerful signal to students. Omission of discourse is not value-neutral education. There is no such thing. Omission is a powerful, even if unintended, signal that these issues are unimportant.

"Granted, the positive results may be impossible to document," wrote former Harvard president Derek Bok in *Beyond the Ivory Tower,*

> But the consequences of doing nothing are plainly intolerable. A university that refuses to take ethical dilemmas seriously violates its basic obligations to society. And a university that fails to engage its members in a debate on these issues and to communicate with care the reasons for its policies gives an impression of moral indifference that is profoundly dispiriting to large numbers of students and professors who share a concern for social issues and a desire to have their institutions behave responsibly. More-

over, any administration that fails to discuss such questions openly and in detail will allow the campus debate on serious moral problems to degenerate into slogans and oversimplification unworthy of an institution dedicated to the rigorous exploration of ideas.[11]

The call to place leadership, ethics, and corporate responsibility at the center of management education is not a plea for heavy-handed indoctrination or other types of misguided behavior. Global competitive pressures are severe. Managers who would rush into the breach between market failures and societal and/or stakeholder needs must understand the legal, competitive, organizational, and fiduciary constraints on any efforts to go beyond corporate economic self-interest.

Instead, this is an effort to suggest a far richer role and responsibility for the manager than that implied by much of management science, so often confined primarily to matter that is empirically demonstrable. This is a call for a deeper sense of purpose, a broader sense of responsibility and accountability, a more proactive spirit, and a more encompassing set of questions, rigorously reasoned. For example,

- On what context does the effective functioning of our democratic capitalistic system depend? Can this system thrive apart from the moral culture that nourishes the virtues and values on which its existence depends? What responsibility do individuals and organizations have to contribute positively to this culture?

- Do markets always "get it right"? What are the appropriate roles for markets, government, and management?

- To whom is a corporation responsible? How are its legitimacy and authority derived? What is the corporation's purpose?

- What responsibility does management have for the stakeholders who constitute the corporate community? How should it weigh competing claims?

- What characteristics do outstanding organizations and
  their leaders exhibit? How important is a reputation for
  reliability, integrity, and fairness? Are the real interests of
  individuals and organizations best served in the long run
  by a systematic refusal to take short-term advantage?
- How can management meet its responsibility to establish—through its choice of systems, structure, and leadership—a corporate context that is consistent with responsible, ethical decisions and actions? How powerful is
  organizational context in determining individual conduct?
- What are our implicit models of human nature? Are we
  stimulated solely by selfishness and greed, or is there
  within each of us a sense of duty and responsibility to
  community?
- How is our individual and collective moral imagination
  formed?
- How should an individual decision maker, confronted
  with an ethical dilemma, reach a decision that is competitively, organizationally, economically, and ethically
  sound?

These are the sorts of questions that collectively define the domain of leadership, ethics, and corporate responsibility—difficult, troubling questions that complicate our already complex and overfilled lives, but that must be addressed and acted
on if the challenges now before us are to be met.

Business Ethics and Management Education

The belief that business education should include discussion of
leadership, ethics, and corporate responsibility has long been
common among those responsible for shaping a business
school curriculum. Robert Gordon and James Howell, in their
1959 landmark report on management education, stated that

"business education must be concerned not only with competence but also with responsibility, not only with skills but also with the attitudes of businessmen," and that "business schools have an obligation to do what they can to develop a 'sense of social responsibility' and a high standard of business ethics in their graduates."[12] Frank Pierson, in a companion report for the Carnegie Corporation, observed that an

> important influence shaping the work of business schools is the increasing attention being given to the social re sponsibilities of business enterprises. Formal standards embodied in law and governmental regulations are but one aspect of this development. Even more pervasive are the informal rules and obligations which the community expects business to meet, whether they involve dealings at national, state, or local levels. No one would argue that there is a clear and precise code of conduct applicable to business in its relations with representatives of government, unions, suppliers, stockholders, rival firms, and the like, but the norms within which employers operate are nonetheless real."[13]

Despite these and subsequent exhortations, leadership, ethics, and corporate responsibility remain peripheral concerns at many, if not most, schools. Surely there have been courageous individual efforts in these areas. The number of "business ethics" and "business and society" courses, the provision of regular conferences, the growing number of textbooks on these topics, and the founding of numerous centers demonstrate that such efforts are very real. Yet often, these activities, like philosophy, have been "remote from the traditional intellectual center of gravity of business education."[14] As Derek Bok explains:

> [F]ew influential voices from our schools of management speak out on issues of corporate responsibility or the role of free enterprise, even though many prominent execu-

tives believe that public attitudes about the corporation's place in society will have a decisive influence on the future of American business. Corporate leaders sometimes complain that academic critics have a bias against business, citing authors such as John Kenneth Galbraith, Charles Lindblom, and Robert Heilbroner. Yet the wonder is not that critics of business exist, but that so few members of the leading management faculties are willing or able to contribute significantly to the debate.[15]

It is undoubtedly true that the very limited progress and absence of voice in some schools are the result of inattention. But this would be an erroneous and unfortunate interpretation of the efforts of many others—unfortunate in its failure to understand the very substantial challenges that have brought disappointment at Harvard and elsewhere, unfortunate because any ethics program, to be successful, must overcome three realities that have frustrated earlier initiatives: the necessity of implementing a broadly based program; the difficulty of gaining broad faculty support and involvement; and the absence, until recently, of any strongly felt need for change.

A Basis for Conversation

In the late 1980s, the situation changed abruptly. Scandal, evidence of rapidly diminishing trust, heightened environmental concerns, excesses associated with deregulation, and fundamental questioning of American practice and competitiveness in the wider global context raised doubts as to the sufficiency of management education and brought issues of leadership, ethics, and corporate responsibility back to the fore.

This book is an explanation of how one business school is trying to place leadership, ethics, and corporate responsibility at the center of its ethos and mission. It is a story of hope and concern, of progress and yet unfinished initiatives. It is a call to rebalance the educational trilogy of values, knowledge, and skills. Each is important; each is insufficient in isolation.

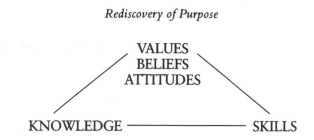

The recommendations and reasoning reflect a substantial and ongoing research and teaching program; but we make no claim to perfection. If that were a prerequisite, this book might never have been written. Nor is this an attempt to identify Harvard Business School as a pioneer, for many schools have undertaken significant efforts to incorporate ethics issues into their educational programs, and Harvard has benefited immeasurably from the outstanding efforts of faculty and administrators and programs past and present, both its own and those of other business schools. Rather, we are attempting to share insights gathered from our intensive efforts over the past five years to better fulfill our fundamental responsibility: that is, to educate professional women and men who possess not only certain basic skills and knowledge, and a broad managerial perspective, but also a heightened sense of the moral and social responsibility their education and future positions of power require. Ultimately, this book is offered in the hope that it will encourage thoughtful, extended, and broad conversation within and among academic institutions and within the corporations that for most of our graduates become the real schools of life—conversation not about what we should "teach," but about the attributes that future leaders must develop if the challenges in the decades ahead are to be met successfully for our children and theirs.

It will never be the case that all students will take from education all of the qualities of character and judgment that they need to perform well in practice. But professional education can imbue some of these qualities, and probably more than it thinks possible. And it can encourage a vision of a career that connects students' work with probity that stirs and moves, troubles and excites.

NOTES

1. Michael L. Dertouzos, Richard K. Lester, and Robert M. Solow, *Made in America* (Cambridge, MA: MIT Press, 1989), p. 99.

2. Gallup Organization: *Gallup Report,* release date December 1988; *Gallup Poll-AIPO,* release date April 9, 1979. Public Opinion Online (data base).

3. Yankelovich and Skelly, *Corporate Priorities,* 1972; Yankelovich, Skelly, and White, release date December 12, 1979. Public Opinion Online (data base).

4. Louis Harris Organization, released February 1966. In Louis Harris, *The Harris Poll,* August 4, 1991. Louis Harris and Associates, released August 4, 1991. Public Opinion Online (data base).

5. Donald L. Kanter and Philip H. Mirvis, *The Cynical Americans: Living and Working in an Age of Discontent and Disillusion* (San Francisco: Jossey-Bass, 1989), p. 2.

6. Kenneth R. Andrews, ed., *Ethics in Practice* (Boston: Harvard Business School Press, 1989), p. 5.

7. Peter J. Neary, "Through a Text Darkly: Business Ethics and the Humanities," in *Ethics in American Business: A Special Report* (Touche Ross & Co.), p. 51.

8. A. Bartlett Giamatti, *The University and the Public Interest* (New York: Atheneum, 1981), p. 10.

9. Scott Turow, *One L* (New York: G. P. Putnam's Sons, 1977), p. 64.

10. John Akers, speech to Bay Area Council (February 10, 1988).

11. Derek Bok, *Beyond the Ivory Tower* (Cambridge, MA: Harvard University Press, 1982), p. 126.

12. Robert A. Gordon and James E. Howell, *Higher Education for Business* (New York: Columbia University Press, 1959), p. 111.

13. Frank C. Pierson et al., *The Education of American Businessmen: A Study of University-College Programs in Business Administration* (New York: McGraw-Hill, 1959), p. 92.

14. Charles W. Powers and David Vogel, *Ethics in the Education of Business Managers* (Hastings-on-Hudson, NY: The Hastings Center, 1980), p. 59.

15. Derek Bok, *Higher Learning* (Cambridge, MA: Harvard University Press, 1986), p. 99.

CHAPTER TWO

Is It Too Late?
Young Adults and the Formation of Professional Ethics

SHARON DALOZ PARKS

Are young adult graduate students, typically in their twenties and early thirties, too old to learn ethics? No. Indeed, there is no time in the human life cycle more strategic for shaping the norms and potential of the moral vision that will ground the ethical choices embedded in the daily decisions and actions of a professional manager. Further, the typical entering student in some of the best MBA programs might be described as more than ready for ethical reflection—in a sense "cheated" of the opportunity to engage in such reflection earlier. The opportunities and responsibilities that rest with business schools and other professional institutions are, therefore, enormous.

Empirical evidence demonstrating the importance of moral education in the young adult years has been charted across the past decade and a half by researchers such as Conry and Nelson, Gandz and Hayes, Bebeau and Rest.[1] This work, together with insights gained from constructive–developmental learning theory and our own study at Harvard Business School, strongly suggests that moral development can continue into adulthood, and that particularly dramatic changes can occur in young adulthood in the context of professional school education. Surely adult moral and ethical development occurs in a variety of settings, both formal and informal, but there is now ample evidence that ethical consciousness and commitment can continue to undergo transformation at least throughout formal education.[2] These findings fly in the face of a good deal of conventional conviction.

The Doubters

"Is it too late?" The question is most often posited rhetorically
by a concerned, weary, and despairing public. To be sure, it is
sometimes raised as a red herring by people who are resistant
to the inclusion of ethics in the business curriculum, and there
are some MBA students who assert, "No one is going to teach
me ethics at this point in my life—I know what I believe."

Conventional thought tends to equate education in ethics
with character formation and thus assumes that ethics cannot
be taught after the age of ten or twelve at the latest, a naive and
dangerous view rooted in the popular psychology of character
formation strongly influenced by Freud. A narrow understanding of Freud's notion that the superego represents the basic structure of morality and is established around the age of
five or six constitutes a form of developmental determinism
that contemporary psychological research does not support.
Less-sophisticated rationales are manifest in such sentimental
romantic notions as "everything is learned at mother's knee."

It cannot be stated too strongly that precursors of adult ethical practice are, indeed, laid down in the early years of life.
Nussbaum, for example, has argued elegantly that "What
Aristophanes saw is that Socrates was indifferent to the antecedent moral training of those he engaged in dialectic." He
mocked "habituation without acknowledging that it might be
essential in forming a pupil's moral intuitions to the point at
which the search for justification can appropriately begin. . . .
pre-rational training must prepare the soul for the full reasoned understanding of virtue."[3] Yet, as has been rightly observed, if in the early childhoods of great lawyers we found
some precursors of verbal aggressiveness and appreciation for
logical argument, and then we identified a verbally aggressive
and more-logical-than-average twenty-year-old, it would be
strange to suggest that a legal education would be unnecessary
for this individual.[4] Talent and basic predispositions are not
enough to enable a person to function effectively as a lawyer in
a courtroom. Likewise, neither is good early-childhood habit-

uation in the moral realm, nor a capacity for empathy, nor "good personal character" sufficient for guiding the decision making of the professional business manager in the contemporary world. Yet, because explicit ethical preparation has been so marginalized in the professions, and the power of early moral training sentimentalized, many cast a jaundiced eye upon efforts to restore ethical commitment to a professional curriculum for young adults—especially when the focus is business education.

Such skepticism is not entirely unwarranted. Documenting scores in principled moral reasoning (which requires the capacity to hold multiple perspectives) across graduate programs, Rest found that students in business ranked lower than did graduate students in moral philosophy and political science, law, medicine, and dentistry.[5] In light of this finding, one might hypothesize that those attracted to business may be predisposed to take a more circumscribed view, leading to a higher-than-average motivation toward self-interest and, specifically, money-making. Indeed, although other potentially lucrative careers (e.g., law and medicine) remain more or less viably connected to public values (justice and health), business, in recent times, does not,[6] or, such undergirding public purpose as is sustained has been markedly eroded in the conventional imagination.[7]

New Realities

Yet two facts of contemporary society are steadily dislodging the naivete, complacency, and cynicism that plague the discussion of ethics in the business curriculum.

1. There has been a steady upsurge of interest in business management, and a concomitant rise in the grade point average of entering students. "In 1970–71, business degrees were roughly one-third as numerous as degrees in the arts and sciences; but in 1984–85, the numbers of degrees were almost equal."[8] Over roughly the same period, that is, between 1969 and 1989, the entering grade

point average at the Harvard Business School rose from
2.7 to 3.5. These figures, even after accounting for
grade inflation and a leveling of these trends, confirm
our more informal perceptions that a significant number
of young adults and a good many of our most academically successful students are seeking careers in business
management.

This dramatic shift is, perhaps, understandable and even appropriate when it is also observed that:

2. "The economy is the dominant institution in modern
   society"[9] and "the large corporation . . . has become the
   definitive institution of modern Western culture. The
   large corporation dominates the modern world in much
   the same way that the church and the university dominated the medieval world."[10] Business managers, being
   key players in these dominant institutions, are increasingly and necessarily expected to exercise public leadership on behalf of the common good across a wide spectrum of fields and issues, ranging from income security
   and health care development and delivery to protection
   of the world's natural environment and financial structures and instruments for both global and domestic
   economies.

In this context, the question "Is it too late?" becomes sober,
crucial speculation, especially when asked by faculty, administrators, and others directly involved with preparing young
adults for careers in the business and other managerial professions (see Chapter One). And it begs another question: Will
these bright young adults, who are pledging their energies to
significant positions in "the definitive institutions" of an increasingly global culture, prove to have the skill, courage, and
vision to practice constructive moral leadership?[11]

Questions and Fears

This small, powerful question—Is it too late?—inevitably
masks additional questions and fears: Do future managers (and

their professors) have to become philosophical ethicists? If we teach ethics, do we have to get involved in religion? How would we do that in a pluralistic, secular culture without becoming sectarian and/or divisive? Does ethical teaching involve indoctrination—and, if so, how can it possibly be a fitting activity in the modern academy? And finally, at the core of this powerful little question so fraught with concern, fear, and cynicism, there lurks also a perception of ethics as a saboteur of the deeply cherished though spurious myth of value-neutral education. Yet all the while, "A business class without ethical undertones has yet to be taught."[12]

Is it too late? An adequate answer to this question is best rooted in every great teacher's most fundamental question: Who are our students?

Who Are Our Students?

The Study: Precedents and Purposes

It behooves every educational institution from time to time to rekindle its curiosity about students themselves—who are they really? Who are our students now in comparison with who our students were a decade or two ago? Every institution develops over time a shared myth about the character of its student body, and the gap between myth and reality can become enlarged and debilitating (for faculty, students, and administrators alike) if this question is not regularly re-engaged in systematic and timely forms.

Harvard Business School has demonstrated more formal and consistent interest in knowing its students than have many graduate professional schools. Charles D. Orth 3d published a major study in 1963, *Social Structure and Learning Climate: The First Year at the Harvard Business School*. Other members of the faculty and administration—e.g., C. Roland Christensen, Abby Hansen, John Kotter, Patricia Light, Margaret McKenna, Quinn Mills, Howard Stevenson, Lewis Ward, and Abraham Zaleznik—likewise have systematically studied and reflected on various aspects of the nature and experience of students during and/or after their two years of MBA study.

As Harvard Business School, along with many other professional schools, began to readdress issues of ethics in its curriculum, it seemed appropriate and even essential that the question "Who are our students?" be re-posed. Accordingly, because of my earlier work with young adult development in the context of higher education, I was invited to join the faculty and administration in a re-examination of this question. This effort has been timely also because it coincides with several significant changes in both student body and curriculum since, for example, the period of the Orth study.

Working directly with Thomas Piper, Senior Associate Dean and head of the Ethics Project; his associate, Senior Research Fellow, Mary Gentile; Earl Sasser, faculty chair of the MBA program; and the faculty teaching the first-year module in ethics, I directed a modest study of first-year students. The effort here has been not so much to study HBS students per se, as to understand young adults in this age cohort who at this time in the life of our society seek graduate education in business management at an outstanding professional school. Therefore two other schools were invited to collaborate, and companion studies have taken place at the Darden School of Business at the University of Virginia (a pioneer in the readdressing of ethics in the business curriculum), directed by Rosalyn Berne with Edward Freeman, and at the Amos Tuck School of Business at Dartmouth, directed by Deborah Chapman with Leonard Greenhalgh. Though the research design has been modified for each school, the correlations in the primary findings across the three schools are strong.

At Harvard, because we wanted to understand as much as possible about who students are when they initially come to the school, we interviewed forty-two students chosen by random sample (about five percent of the entering class) during the first six weeks of the academic year (1989–1990). Thirty-four of these same students were interviewed again in April and May. I conducted most of the interviews, which were from one to two hours in duration.[13] I was identified simply as a visiting professor working with Piper and Sasser in an effort to understand students in relationship to ongoing curricular revision. Students were told that their identity would remain confidential, that they were not being studied as individuals per se but rather as representatives of the wider student body, yet they were expected to speak only for themselves. The interviews were tape recorded and transcribed, then analyzed both by me and by a second reader, Karen Thorkilsen. In preparation for these interviews, I consulted with a number of key faculty and administrators to solicit input from a variety of perspectives in formulating both hypotheses and interpretations.

In sum, we found that these talented, highly motivated students have a strong sense of interpersonal accountability—of being trustworthy—in immediate face-to-face situations with colleagues and superiors. Yet perhaps because many of them have been insulated from diversity and failure, and have not heretofore been encouraged to critically reflect upon some of the important issues before them and their societies, they only have a limited consciousness of systemic harm and injustice, only a limited sense of what is at stake. As a consequence, most do not yet articulate a vision by which they believe they could positively affect our collective life—signaling an absence of worthy myths and dreams. Unless they are effectively initiated into the public purposes and ethical norms of their profession, they will be ill-prepared to provide managerial leadership capable of engaging complex relationships among conflicting loyalties within a vision of the common good. They will not be able to provide ethical leadership in public life.

Grounding Hypotheses: Forms of Meaning-Making

The initial hypotheses came from my earlier work,[14] grounded in the constructive-developmental perspectives of Mead,

Dewey, Piaget, Kohlberg, Perry, Keniston, Kegan, Fowler, Selman, and Gilligan. This tradition takes seriously the fact of the composing human mind. This tradition recognizes that all human beings continually reorder their sense of self, world, and ultimate reality. Further, predictable patterns of growth in the capacity to manage greater degrees of complexity in moral reasoning can be identified. These patterns (described by some theorists as stages or balances) emerge from the prior activity of making meaning. This meaning-making activity is an inter-active process and thus is dependent upon and stimulated by the conditions in the environment. Meaning-making is a pro-cess of seeking order, pattern, and significance.

All human beings make meaning at what might be called mundane levels—making sense out of our immediate context, composing patterns by which we move through and interpret the events of every day. But human beings do not seem to settle for making meaning merely at the level of the mundane. Human beings require meaning of the whole. We seek to understand the wider purposes and significance of the largest frame of existence we can conceive of. We reserve the word "faith" for the activity of making meaning in its most compre-hensive dimensions—dimensions that embrace all that is ulti-mate and most intimate. Thus the activity of faith is strongly related to the conditions of ultimate trust and value (whether expressed in religious or secular terms). Faith, therefore, is not necessarily religious. It is something that all human beings do in the lifelong, everyday meaning-making that happens in the dialectic between fear and trust, alienation and belonging, hope and hopelessness, power and powerlessness.[15]

Finally, and most crucial for the discussion here, it is vital to recognize that the patterns and contents of meaning-making in its most comprehensive dimensions (faith) form the ground of moral choice; for while we may or may not act in a manner consistent with what we say we value and believe, human beings will act so as to align themselves with what is perceived to be ultimately true, trustworthy, and dependable. Human beings will behave in a manner that is consistent with the construction held "deep in the gut" to be the actual reality of things—what seems to finally count. For most of us, there are significant shifts from time to time in how we make meaning, in how we compose our convictions of ultimate reality. Accordingly, our behavior may shift over time. Education— that is, coming to see in a new way—may precipitate such a shift.[16]

Thus we were concerned in this study of the entering MBA students with the forms of their meaning-making, because this is our best clue as to how they will ground their day-to-day decision making—with all of its moral, ethical ramifications. To this end, we were curious about such matters as their definitions of success, what they were concerned about, how they perceived their world, and what issues seemed important as they anticipated their own personal futures. To illustrate, if we were to find that students believe—as do many practicing managers—that responsible business decision making is ultimately and best oriented to quarterly earnings and shareholder returns, we know that those values will bear significant influence in shaping their ethical stance—their workaday faith. (We found that indeed these values are salient, but are held within a configuration of additional significant values.)

My earlier work also suggested that these MBA students (all of typical young adult age, twenty-four to thirty-two, and graduates of four years of higher education) would demonstrate a significant measure of critical thought. They would have moved beyond reflective, but uncritical, and primarily interpersonal forms of reflection upon life (see Appendix). Reflective, interpersonal adult thought typically emerges in the teen-age years—and can, indeed, be sustained without further development throughout all of adult life. This form of thought gives one the power to move beyond concrete thought into more aware and abstract thought and to use metaphor, symbol, and some forms of complex logic. But this form of thought is finally dependent upon authority outside the self (e.g., the media, cultural traditions, professors, and the like); thus it holds broad cultural assumptions and beliefs in a tacit, uncritical manner—assuming that things just are as they are or that someone else understands and takes care of whatever apparent contradictions or mysteries may appear. Thus the world of immediate interpersonal relationships and transactions are the primary locus of engagement and reflection when one thinks and acts in this conventional, authority-bound mode rooted in tacitly held assumptions—even if one plays a social role characterized as having a high level of "independence," power, and responsibility.

If, however, one bumps up against enough contradictions, moments of dissonance, and experiences that just don't fit one's assumptions, one may change one's mind.[17] A new way of seeing may be composed; one may make meaning in a new form and consequently behave in some new ways. One may begin to wonder more about why things are as they are and if they have to be that way. One may begin to think about one's own thinking—and how it is conditioned by time and place. One may no longer so easily just presume "Authority knows" and may instead begin to take responsibility for knowing for oneself—even at the level of ultimate reality. If this occurs, one begins to practice a more critical, self-aware, and systemic form of thought. One becomes more inner-dependent (though still taking the views of others into account). One may continue to value interpersonal reality but simultaneously hold more systemic awareness—whether the focus be, for example, social, financial, or procedural.[18]

Further, what I found through earlier study and research (informed in part by the work of Kenneth Keniston, now of MIT) was a significant step (or stage) in the journey from Authority-bound and interpersonal forms of thought and meaning-making to critical-systemic modes of meaning-making. We are beginning to recognize a new stage in the human life cycle, a place in between (adolescent-adult) uncritical, interpersonal thought and (more mature adult) critical-systemic thought.[19] This place is potentially characteristic of young adulthood, the twenties and perhaps the early thirties.

In young adulthood one may have developed a genuinely critical perspective on self and world, yet remain appropriately dependent upon worthy mentors and mentoring environments in the further formulation of tested adult perceptions and commitments (see Appendix).

Thus it was hypothesized that the entering MBA students, in light of their age, intelligence, education, work, and travel experience, would manifest critical, self-aware systemic thought. They would have a significant measure of inner dependence in their modes of meaning–making, yet would be appropriately dependent upon mentors and mentoring communities in their ongoing formation into full adult responsibilities and competencies. A counter hypothesis, offered by a few seasoned members of the Harvard Business School faculty, was that despite their obvious talent, education, work experience, and sophistication, many of these students (for various reasons that we will describe) might actually be found to be "younger" and more dependent upon authorities and contexts outside the self than one might assume. That is, when viewed through this developmental perspective, the entering students might tend toward the reflective and interpersonal rather than the critical and systemic end of the spectrum. With these hypotheses and counter hypotheses in hand, as well as some questions specific to the ethics module and curriculum at Harvard, we proceeded with the interviews.

Many months of listening, analysis, and reflection later, the seasoned faculty proved to be most accurate in their perceptions. Why?

The Flow of Success

The average age of the students when they enter the school is twenty-six. As a group, they are highly motivated, talented, and bright. Most are graduates of the best secondary and undergraduate schools. Many of the American students, upon graduation from college, were recruited and subsequently trained by some of our most prestigious commercial and financial institutions or by the military. (Some international students share a similar profile, albeit in the context of their respective countries.[20]) It is a well-publicized fact that upon graduation from the MBA program, many of these young adult students will secure positions paying $70,000 per year and more. Some left even higher salaries to pursue their master's degree. They typically do not expect to return to the particular organization they have been with, not out of any specific complaint so much as some intuition that there is something more or better for them elsewhere. Only a small percentage of them come from elite families, but as a group they do come predominantly from upwardly mobile middle-class backgrounds. Our society seems to work for them.

From some angles of vision, these young adults obviously represent a certain sort of privilege. Yet this particular profile of young adult success seems to have a number of implications that are soberingly significant in terms of the students' potential as future managers and leaders. Specifically, because they have been in this "flow of success," many of them have had less occasion for critical reflection on self and world than have others their age. Most are fully capable of critical thought and can employ it to work out a strategy within a given set of conditions. But in the absence of significant adversity and/or cross-cultural cognitive dissonance, they have had less experience than have some of their generational peers in recognizing and considering the conditions themselves—the broader social, cultural, political, and economic context within which the conditions themselves rest. Therefore they remain more vulnerable than might be presumed to the unexamined assumptions of conventional thought and circumstance.

Vacuous Credos

One of the forms in which this vulnerability to conventional thought is manifest resides in the phenomenon we have described as "vacuous credos." Many students came in the door, as it were, repeatedly espousing such credos as "The important thing is to act—whether you are right or wrong," or "I must do my personal best." The implications of these credos tend to flow something like this:

INTERVIEWER: When all is said and done, what would you like your life ultimately to be about?
STUDENT: I would like to achieve my personal goals.
INTERVIEWER: What might some of those be?
STUDENT: I guess that would depend on what company I was with.
INTERVIEWER: What kind of company would you like to work with?
STUDENT: It wouldn't really matter.

At first hearing, these statements appear devoid of substantive interest or commitment. Over the course of both rounds of interviews, however, we have come to respect that these vacuous credos do not, in fact, reveal a total absence of substantive values. In some cases, it is true, we must conclude that the primary values are those of achieving success, however it is defined by the prevailing culture, with little self-reflective choice. And if this is the case, we must assume that such students are extremely vulnerable to becoming the victims of unconsidered and inadequate goals.[21] Yet in response to most of the interviews, we must conclude that these vacuous credos signal that these young adults have been upwardly mobile in a culture that is both individualistic and pluralistic. That is, doing one's personal best and achieving one's personal goals are values that are both socially confirmed and socially inoffensive in a pluralistic context—in other words, a context in which articulating the full substance of one's value commitments might create tensions that would inhibit the upward flow of success.

Some of these same young adults, however, seem to hold deeply cherished values such as the dignity of all persons and the importance of integrity and compassion, or a commitment to working on behalf of a specific social issue. Many of these

147642

students not only hold such values, they have acted in specific situations in ways that are dramatically congruent with those commitments. But like many in our society (including those older than they), they do not yet appear to have at hand a publicly legitimized, comfortable language whereby they might forthrightly and gracefully articulate those commitments. The implication here is that without an adequate public language, ethical commitments tend to remain a matter of personal (or privatized) morality and are thus rendered impotent for social and corporate transformation.[22] At a time when our society seeks a fresh, bold, and credible articulation of grounding and compelling ethical principles, many of these students are well motivated, but they are not yet adequately prepared to articulate their values in the service of ethical leadership whether in the classroom, the company, or our wider public life.

Morality: An Interpersonal Matter

The dominance of an interpersonal or privatized sense of morality (in contrast to a more public, systemic ethical awareness) is evident in other forms as well. It is perhaps most vividly portrayed in a response to one of the last questions we asked in the first interview: "You have commented on some of the things you would like to accomplish; as you think across all of the years ahead, who do you think you may hurt?" Because we presumed that the typical student would not have thought much about the question, students were given ample time to consider it. After a pause, the typical response was, "I hope I won't hurt anybody." When the interviewer, with a questioning look, provided more time, the student might add, "I might hurt my family." If the interviewer with a questioning look provided yet more time, the student might then say, "Well, I might have to fire somebody." The sense conveyed by this last response is that the student might be faced with the unhappy prospect of terminating the employment of a single individual—an interpersonal situation. Yet these students typically expect to have positions of significant responsibility in very major companies, or to head their own (large and successful) businesses. Thus, although these young adults tend to have a strong sense of interpersonal accountability (e.g., being trustworthy) in immediate face-to-face situations with colleagues and superiors,[23] they do not yet seem to have a correspondingly clear consciousness of systemic hurt and injustice and its relationship to their own action in the world (both present and future). While this interpretation requires further study, it now appears that they do not readily recognize that some of them have already made, and many of them will make, complex decisions that may affect hundreds or even thousands of people whom they will never see and/or aspects of the ecosystem not immediately evident. Thus when a student says, "No one can teach me ethics; I know what is right and wrong," it appears that he or she speaks primarily with reference to an interpersonal ethical frame.

An interpersonal ethic of trustworthiness and mutual accountability is essential but not sufficient for ethical managerial practice. The moral imagination of young adults moving into corporations may be constrained by the limitations of the interpersonal model, rendering them vulnerable to the potential traps of personal ambition and "company loyalty," narrowly defined, and leaving them insufficiently prepared to exert managerial leadership capable of addressing the complex and interdependent relationships among competing claims within a vision of the common good. They will not be prepared adequately to create a positive corporate culture within which other decision makers will function.

Readiness for Initiation into Complexity and Ambiguity

In light of the preceding observations, it is significant that the response of these students as a group to the required ethics module (taught in the first four weeks of the academic year) was very positive. After considering from an ethical perspective nine typical management cases across the regular functional areas of the MBA curriculum (see Chapter Three), students were stimulated by the complexity and ambiguity involved in the ethical dimensions of the managerial decision-making process. Remarked one twenty-six-year-old male student:

> It changed the way I was viewing the role of the business-man. . . . I was probably above the average in terms of sensibility towards human and environmental issues. . . . It probably enhanced my sense of the impact my decisions as a business leader . . . upon the community as defined very, very broadly . . . not just increasing my shareholder value, but being part of a much broader system which includes countries, cities, local communities . . . and understanding that whatever decision I make can have an impact which can go much further than just increasing the bottom line. . . . I have to balance the interests of the different parts of the whole system.

The encounter with ambiguity was reflected in the comments of many students, including those of a twenty-seven-year-old woman who remarked:

> I'm very hard-line, straight and level when it comes to an ethical choice. There's black and white. . . . But here we're being challenged with, "Yes, there's an obvious right and wrong, maybe, when it comes to a personal choice [but] when it comes to a business you have other decisions; other stakeholders, other people are involved, and you have to think about every segment when you're making this decision and the effects that it will have." . . . And so, in my mind, I see a lot more gray than I did before, and I find it very uncomfortable.

A twenty-seven-year-old male expressed his learning this way:

> Before, [when] I looked at a problem in the business world I never consciously examined the ethical issues in play. It was always subconscious and I hope that I somewhat got it. But that [ethics] was never even a considera-

tion. But now, when I look at a problem, I have to look at the impact. I'm going to put in this new ten-million-dollar project. What's going to be the impact on the people that live in the area and the environment? And what's a long-term risk to the water supply here that the public is using? It's opened my mind up on those things. It's also made me more aware of situations where I might be walking down the wrong path and getting in deeper and deeper, to where I can't pull back.

And a twenty-five-year-old student said, "I do think it's possible [to teach ethics] because I learned a ton." These comments are representative of most students in our sample. Even those students to whom it seemed important to maintain the you-won't-teach-people-new-morality conviction simultaneously affirmed that they, along with the others, gained a broader perspective. Remarked one twenty-five-year-old:

I honestly don't know if I have learned a whole lot different about ethics; but . . . the difference has been the level of analysis, when you think about who are all the people involved, who gets hurt the most, and who is my primary responsibility. . . . I'm not sure I thought through those things as systematically before I came here as I do now.

Thus the module seemed to serve most students as an initiation into a more complex frame of ethical reflection, an initiation for which they appear to be more than ready. In other words, they appear to have been ready for this kind of reflection for some time, but it has not been asked of many of them.

It is not too late. It is time.

Vulnerability to the Conventional Ethos

Without an initiation into critical reflection upon self and upon the systemic complexity and ambiguity these students will be expected to manage, we expect that many of them will continue to subscribe to whatever conventional ethos prevails—as long as they are successful within it. As one professor observed, they are vulnerable to being "context driven." Indeed, one value of the ethics module, according to some students, was that it enabled them to

> put themselves in [the case] situation and say "we did that all the time" and "I shouldn't have done that. . . . I wasn't thinking" and see the benefit of pulling back and really observing what you're doing and why. . . . People would say, "Oh my, you know, we used to load up inventory and have it sit at the end of the parking lot so we could register it for sales. They used to do that all the time to make our end of the quarter figures look good." Or people would talk about [how they had been] kind of stepping over the line without having realized it was stepping over the line.

In the light of this student (indeed, human) vulnerability to context, it is important and useful to consider the nature of the conventional ethos in which most of these students dwell.

Noblesse Oblige

Some students come from families and/or schools in which the tradition of noblesse oblige plays an influential role. Thus these students can anticipate career paths where their responsibility to "do good" begins *after* achieving certified success (defined, at least in part, in monetary terms). Those who dwell in this ethos can derive a sort of permission to postpone serious consideration of how they might do good in the meantime. A tendency to separate the "how" by which success is generated from an ethic of care for a wider public is also implicit in this set of assumptions. Particularly for those who do not stand in this tradition as a family inheritance (the majority) and for those who appear not to have had good early-childhood habituation in the moral realm (a small but real minority), this prevailing norm of postponement leaves a vacuum that can foster vulnerability first to the "conventions of respectability" but also to the "conventions of fear and greed" or, more frequent and subtle, simply to the norms of consumerism. For example, when asked, "How much money would be enough?" the typical respondent answered, "Enough to support my lifestyle." For most, "lifestyle" was defined by the norms of material success in the culture. (No one mentioned the category of "need," although two spoke of a "floor of security" and two others volunteered, "I will probably always have a lifestyle to match my income.") It was difficult to ascertain at what point the typical student would decide that enough "noblesse" had been achieved to set in motion the activity of "oblige." In any case, this venerable tradition leaves many young adult future managers unchallenged and in effect disempowered as moral agents in the present. What this tradition perhaps best serves is an ethic of philanthropy, which is a significant but limited aspect of what is intended when we speak of decision making, ethical values, and corporate responsibility.

Masking Failure

Another feature of these students' prevailing ethos is presumed success and a consequent masking of failure. In the second interview, a twenty-five-year-old who had been successful in a major consulting firm described the corporate culture, in part, in these terms: "There was definitely an attitude in the office that you cannot admit that you made a mistake, that [you] should not admit that you were wrong, or that you didn't know something." We posed the following comment and question to each student: "Most people who come here, including yourself, have achieved a good measure of success in their lives; but no life is a hundred percent success. Can you remember a time when you experienced a significant measure of disappointment, discouragement, or failure?" With few exceptions, students could not identify, even with some substantial prodding, any such experience.

Since these students are relatively young and have been in environments that basically work for them, the absence of significant discouragement, disappointment, or failure is neither totally surprising nor disturbing. What is significant is that some were quite candid in conveying that they thought it would be difficult for them even to recognize failure in their life. These students seem to have a sense of being buffered from such possibilities, or, perhaps more accurately, they appear to carry the burden of so managing their experience as to maintain the perception (in their own eyes as well as in those of others) of never failing.[24] They face careers in which risk taking is an admired norm of leadership, yet the possibility of failure seemed to them remote if not unimaginable.

This observation suggests that they are vulnerable to an unstated but marked "ethic of control" that pervades much of their conventional ethos.[25] This is to say that their understanding of the "good" may be shaped in significant measure by what will ensure a positive flow of events, success, and security—and thwart at least the appearance of failure. The risk is that these young adults may develop a sort of "armor," an inextricably vested interest in being a "success" despite what that may mean for others.

This dynamic is particularly significant in the face of Abraham Zaleznik's controversial but suggestive thesis that leaders are people who have suffered significant and painful conflict, who have endured major events that have led to an inward turning and even estrangement from their environments, from which they have emerged with a "created rather than an inherited sense of identity."[26] Such experience fosters critical reflection on the conditions of things and enables the individual to imagine in visionary terms and take genuine risks, thereby providing leadership toward constructive change. If we subscribe to this thesis, a young adult who is vulnerable to a conventional ethos that assumes a career of avoiding or eluding painful conflict and failure would not be a candidate for significant managerial leadership.

Business as a Game

Another mark of the conventional ethos shared by these young adults is the metaphor of "game" as a way of talking about business.[27] The author's earlier work recognized that meaning-making and its ethical-moral consequences are shaped not only by the formal structures of knowing (i.e., interpersonal or systemic), but also by the content—the language, images, metaphors—those structures hold.[28] An interpersonal orientation to ethics is thus shaped in part, for example, by whether one thinks of the corporation to which one is loyal primarily as a "family," a "team," a "community," or an "organization." The team and game metaphors are pervasive in the professional business ethos in which these young adults participate and to which they aspire. These metaphors are strengthened by widespread participation in sports and physical fitness, which are dominant and highly visible values in the contemporary business-school ethos, at the corporate board meeting, and in commercial sponsorship of community and professional athletics. Sports and fitness can and do make major contributions to personal and social health; yet when these metaphors are used without self-conscious, critical reflection in relationship to business as a profession, they may render superficial the issues at stake in business transactions or foster a competitive (and sometimes exhilarating) intensity that may blind individuals (or groups) to the consequences of their choices and actions. There is evidence that some dubious ethical choices are justified under the rubric "It's part of the business game."[29]

The game orientation, like the interpersonal orientation, presumes a limited frame of reference, a circumscribed playing field in which only particular rules apply—and in which certain behaviors may be tolerable that would otherwise be unacceptable.[30] Game metaphors, because they generally do not acknowledge the sobering consequences embedded in most major commercial and financial decisions and transactions, ironically serve to insulate the "players" from the implications of their actions in the "real world."[31]

Separate Domains of Knowing

Another central feature of living in an ethos characterized by an uncritical dependence on assumed authorities is that, in the absence of critical reflection, mutually contradictory basic life assumptions may go unnoticed. This condition obtains largely because connections between different domains are simply unrecognized. The absence of connections, particularly between differing societal domains, was evident in the response of students who, for example, thought it very important to pay greater attention to the natural environment but believed that business could offer little or no leadership in doing so. Similarly, it was easy for most students to assume a privileged material lifestyle for themselves while expressing concern for the conditions of the growing underclass—never suggesting any relationship between the two. While many were active in volunteer work with social programs such as soup kitchens, tutoring, and property refurbishment (all interpersonal modes of contributing to society), few seemed to possess a critical, self-aware understanding of the systemic dynamics that give rise to the need for such programs. Such interpretations as they had at hand did not typically represent the sort of informed, critical thought of which these students are very capable.

As a consequence, the connections often were not made between espoused political-social-philosophical values and the actual conditions of experience, leading to further contradictions (in a manner that did not suggest an appreciation of complexity so much as an absence of reflection). Some, for example, assumed education to be the answer to ameliorating the conditions of the underclass. Yet they also assumed that education was the responsibility of the government and that government should be as limited as possible. When asked if they thought they would participate in shaping the future, they were likely to assert that they would be able to exert more influence on the future if they went into politics and government. At the same time, they had little respect for the political domain. (Although this perspective might be considered a norm within the conventional business ethos in contemporary American society, it should also be noted that several students, when asked directly about the appropriate relationship between business and government, expressed considerable ambivalence or reconsideration of this question.)

Cynicism

Our findings relative to the student perceptions of government bear on the broader issue of political cynicism as a hallmark of the current generation. Students were asked in our initial interviews to comment on the growing cynicism in our society—especially among those who are *under* thirty-four, a cynicism documented in a recent study by Kanter and Mirvis, *The Cynical Americans: Living and Working in an Age of Discontent and Disillusion.*[32] In general, the business school students we studied do not identify themselves as cynical because they have a positive sense of hope about their personal futures. Nevertheless, it is quite clear that many do tend to be cynical about government and other large institutions, and many of them appear to be best described as apolitical. Some are aware that such cynicism serves as a means of forming community with others in the face of their shared insight into "how the political system, corporation, university, or other large institution really works," and their simultaneous sense of powerlessness and discouragement in relationship to such institutions.

It is important to recognize that these twenty-six-year-olds were about ten years old and coming to a rudimentary political awareness at the time of Watergate, so we should, perhaps, not be surprised by their political cynicism. Moreover, most of them cannot remember when our streets held few who were homeless or otherwise alienated from the social franchise.

Some seem to believe that things are as they always have been—and always will be. Therefore it appears to be in relationship to our connected-collective-common public life, in contrast to their individual lives, that these students have the least hope and feel the least sense of potential competence and efficacy.

In his 1980 report to the Carnegie Foundation, *When Dreams and Heroes Died*,[33] Arthur Levine described a generation of students entering graduate schools and the professions not so much because they hoped to make a positive contribution to the shaping of their world, but in the hope that they would be able to achieve a safe oasis in a world they expected to get worse and which they believed they could not affect.[34] Despite the fact that volunteerism appears to be on the rise among these young adults as in the wider society, these students essentially corroborate the findings of Levine's study. They are confident about their own personal futures, they are not indifferent to "doing good," but most do not yet articulate a vision or strategy by which they believe they could effect significant positive change in our collective life.

Young Adults in Historical Context

Today's students, though seemingly apolitical and described by some as ahistorical,[35] do not dwell in a vacuum. Rather, they mirror quite faithfully the central features of their culture and time, a time that has been described as "between stories."[36] As many of the myths and dreams that used to define a sense of purpose, significance, and direction have eroded for the modern, secular person, we as a culture have become trapped in the concrete. Is it appropriate to berate young adults for being materialistic and greedy at a point in time when their culture has little to offer them besides money and position as symbols of authority, affirmation, success, and belonging? Have not some of our most talented young adults been taught (implicitly, if not explicitly) to define success first in the form of academic grades and then simply to substitute dollar signs for grades—adding vacuous symbols to vacuous credos?

It should not surprise us that a generation for which the unifying myths of cultural purpose are shifting or dissolving is perceived by some as lacking a defining, purpose-orienting event. Many generations have been tested, defined, and directed by a single, shared, pivotal circumstance—an economic depression, a war, an assassination.[37] In contrast, it has been suggested that the defining event of this generation is "isolation." In the same vein, those who are now our students have been described as "iron lung children."[38]

Insulation and Individualism

It is ironic that the generation of young adults that stands on the frontier of a new interdependent globalism should represent new forms of cultural insulation and individualism. At the same time that our social culture is being increasingly homogenized by the media and McDonald's (among the many other informational and commercial networks we all share), we are experiencing isolation by economic class as a growing phenomenon in American society.[39] Today's students, like many of us, do not have much direct experience of people who dwell in an economic stratum and culture other than their own, wherever they are on the economic scale. They can understandably remark, as did one interviewee, that something "in excess of 100K is necessary just to be comfortable in this society." What is manifest here is a very particular definition of "comfortable" and "society," and an ignorance of others' definitions of the same.

What is increasingly shared across economic strata is a form of cultural insulation and a consequent ignorance of one another, of the connections among us, and how, in fact, each economic class is interdependent with and profoundly affects the lives of those in others, both within and beyond national boundaries.[40] This cultural insulation, which may also be described as a form of provincialism,[41] delimits compassion—

the capacity to see (and, if necessary, to suffer) through the
eyes of another. Because compassion is the taproot of the ethical imagination,[42] this is a profoundly disturbing trend. This
cultural insulation similarly delimits the capacity to manage an
emerging global interdependence.

These conditions are exacerbated by the vestiges of the values that have shaped our ethical norms in the past. One of
these is the enormous value we have placed upon the individual. This is not a mistake, but in today's increasingly interdependent world it can become a liability. As artist, writer, and
critic Suzi Gablik has observed, "Individuality and freedom
are undoubtedly the greatest achievements of modern culture.
They have been crucial steps in the development of human
consciousness: we have emerged from simple instinctive or reactive consciousness and have the capacity to transcend the
tribal mind."[43] But we have fallen into the trap of individual*ism*
as an ideology, pushing the values of autonomy, personal
competence, achievement, and freedom to an edge that now
frightens rather than empowers us. We have lost sight of the
relationships between the individual and the social system, between freedom and responsibility. Individual fulfillment for
most is dependent upon a place in a community—some meaningful form of sociality. Our young adults—even some of
those most talented and gifted—are coping with only half of
what they need. They have a vision of freedom to pursue individual contentment. (Many, for example, remarked that
their parents just wanted them to "be happy.") Typically, however, they do not have a correspondingly robust vision of social engagement and responsibility; moreover, they do not yet
have a connective, interdependent imagination by which they
can creatively address the intensifying complexity of an interdependent global economy and ecology.[44] They can see the individual and the individual corporation; they do not as readily
recognize the social-ecological-political fabric within and on
which both must dwell and depend. They do not recognize the
intricate dynamics that constitute the rich interdependence

that they are subject to and that they will shape. They do not yet recognize the interdependent complexity that, when seriously considered, confounds their too-narrowly framed interpersonal ethical resolve.

Understanding Political Socioeconomic Systems

Another noteworthy feature of the inherited historical ethos that forms the conventional ethical orientation of these young adults is not simply an absence of systemic thought, but specifically their yet limited understanding of economic systems. Many in the humanities and the arts acknowledge that they do not understand the complexities of either micro or macro economics, but they presume (perhaps inappropriately) that those in the commercial world have reasonably sophisticated understandings of our economic system. We discovered that generally this is not so for those entering MBA programs. When asked whether they think our economic system should remain the same or be changed, these students tended to respond in the conventional code language of "capitalism versus socialism," "trickle-down economics," and "market forces." They responded at a mythic level, without further analytic nuance.

Most think the present economic system—presumed to be more or less a laissez-faire capitalism—is fine as it is. They seem to have had little occasion to examine, or to even see, interrelationships between systems—for example, between economics and politics or between business and law. This strongly suggests that they have not critically reflected on the character of human nature or the power and limitations of markets, governments, managers, and stockholders.

Among the same students who perceived our economic system to be essentially fine, there were several who (in another portion of the interview) expressed considerable concern about the growing tolerance for the notion of a *permanent underclass* (a concept that runs counter to traditional American democratic and religious traditions). When asked what might be done about this contradiction, few had any idea—even though most of them aspire to such positions of responsibility as CEO of a major corporation. Again, their sense of power as individuals (or at least their sense of power as individuals in the role of CEO) seems to be constrained by the limits of an interpersonal imagination; they express little sense of power or imagination in relationship to the socioeconomic fabric of their wider public life. As their generation stands on the threshold of significant new challenges from Asian economies, a unifying Europe, and a reordering of the former Soviet political and economic order, these students await initiation into a more adequate and precise articulation of the dynamics and goals of democratic capitalism. They appear to engage business in an interpersonal mode, as yet unaware of the systemic reach of their personal energy, both actual and potential.

A Rupture in Western Culture

The split between commerce and social responsibility in the value constructs of these young adults is fostered in part by the rupture in Western culture between material and transcendent values: between the commercial world and the worlds of religion, education, the humanities, and the domicile—including personal and family life. Thus the commercial sector can harbor the pragmatic norm of "you've got to do what you've got to do," with the presumption that the other sectors will preserve and protect the humanizing values of civilization.[45] The commercial world perceives the "humanizing sector" as a haven from the cut and thrust of the business world, but a haven grateful that there is "someone else to do the dirty work." Little recognition of the positive "vocation" of business is articulated within the wider social fabric, a condition that was perhaps tolerable when the business culture was less dominant within society, or more effectively counterbalanced by such institutions as religion and the university.[46] It becomes less tolerable in light of the current reordering of cultural life.

These two worlds—of commerce and of "values"—are each beginning to recognize that our economic-commercial life pervades all sectors of society in a mutually interdependent relationship. But until this fundamental rupture is healed, the subject of "business ethics," if it is to mean something more than the mere conventions of corporate etiquette, is necessarily a problematic category in the conventional mind. The entering MBA student is inevitably influenced by this cultural split, as was evident in several instances in which students expressed the perception that if something was a good business decision (i.e., good for profits), it did not, therefore, "count" or qualify as an ethical decision.

Relationship to the Future

In light of these students' cultural location and consequent potential for leadership and social influence,[47] it was deemed important to explore also their relationship to history and the future. We found them to be less aware that they live in a time of profound historical shifts than we expected. When we asked these students, for example, to comment on their image of the future two generations hence, a third of them indicated that this was something they do not think about. Said one: "I never really thought about that, I live on a more day-to-day basis." And a thirty-one-year-old male, married with one child, said: "Well, I have to tell you I haven't ever really given it much thought. . . . I can't think past Monday!"

Although most students were able to bring some reflection to the question of the future, the images they offered tended to be vague extensions of the present. Several either presumed or hoped that things would remain essentially as they are: "Well," said one, "if they could have what we have now, I think that would be fine. I'm really satisfied with the way things are." The images of most, however, signaled four areas of awareness relative to the future: (1) the assumption that we will have more technology (with varying opinions as to whether this was positive or negative); (2) a related concern that life will become more complex; (3) a particular consciousness of global complexity—played out in either economic, political, or ecological issues, with some seeing positive and others fearing negative consequences; and (4) an awareness of economic disparity—"the deterioration of our cities," "countries will be poor," "income differential will continue to spread . . . almost two societies"—leading, thought some, to more dangerous conditions, or, as others hoped, to things getting better (probably through crises).

Most significant, these students (as we noted earlier) are at best ambivalent about whether they can play a part in shaping a positive future. When asked, for example, "What would you like to have happen during the next fifty years for society?" one twenty-four-year-old male responded: "I guess I would have trouble answering that, I haven't really thought of what objectives I would have."

It is in this sense—that most seem not to have been asked to think beyond the assumed norms of their present world—that these bright, talented, and educationally privileged young adults seem "cheated." They have a very limited sense of what is at stake, what might be feared and/or hoped for, what new risks and opportunities lie on their horizon. They seem not to have had mentors—or, more powerfully, mentoring communities—that could confirm and challenge the promise of their young adult lives and beckon them toward an informed, positive, and compelling vision of the future.

Relationship to History

Though their visions of the future are in certain ways limited, these young adults are not unaffected by historical events. Indeed, while we had to agree with the perception of some commentators that no single "defining historical event" has been powerful enough to galvanize a common sense of identity and purpose for this generation, intuitively it seemed unlikely that a whole population of bright young people remained unaffected by any of the events in their historical period. Thus, at the beginning of the second interview we asked these students to indicate the degree to which they had been affected by some of the events and trends that had occurred in their lifetime. Then we briefly discussed with them their responses and found that almost all recognized some event or events as significant to them. But the choice of event(s) was highly dependent upon social-economic-geographical location, corroborating the notion of isolation or insulation discussed earlier. In this instance, isolation clearly does not mean unaffected. These students clearly were affected by events, but their experience was typically expressed in a privatized form of meaning, conveying little sense of an experience held in common with a people—with the wider human community. This finding suggests that the ground upon which to cultivate a sense of responsibility to the common good is limited.

Nevertheless, these students do seem to hold some common historical experience: eighty-eight percent indicated that they were affected some or a great deal by the entry of women into the work force, the Iran hostage crisis, the release of Mandela, the rise in ecological awareness, and the changes in Eastern Europe and the USSR. When asked which events had affected their peers some or a great deal, ninety-four percent or more added the following: the rise in the divorce rate; AIDS; the crash of 1987; the increase in illegal drugs and crime; the insider trading scandals; and Tiananmen Square. The three events that stood out overall in the perception of this group of students were the entry of women into the work force, the rise in ecological awareness, and the changes in Eastern Europe and the former USSR.

The greatest consensus was around the changes in Eastern Europe and the former USSR. Although the choice of these events may have resulted from the coincidence of their timing with the interview, other world events coincident with the interview did not begin to draw a similar consensus. One occurrence that must be considered in assessing these findings is that three months before this second round of interviews (which took place in the spring of 1990) the school suspended regular classes for two days to focus on events in Eastern Europe and their implications for business management. It is a reasonable hypothesis that, for this generation of students, this focus in the curriculum constituted an act of mentoring on the part of the school, contributing to awareness, identity, and some transcendence of the historical-cultural insulation that marks these students' lives. It should also be noted that the first-year curriculum in Organizational Behavior had directed attention earlier to the significance of the presence of women in the classroom and the work force, and likewise may have influenced students' responses.

Between Generations

From a broad historical perspective, the students we interviewed at the threshold of a new decade appear to represent a transitional moment between generations. They dwell on the cusp between the "boomer" generation[48] of hippies, yuppies, and Wall Street tycoons and the dramatically smaller "bust" generation that now follows them. The so-called bust generation is said to disdain the yuppies, assume a more limited economic-material opportunity, and feel it has inherited a mess of social ills it will have to remedy, though it is motivated by neither the social idealism of the hippies nor the economic expectations of the yuppies.[49] In contrast, the entering MBA students we interviewed, like the boomers before them, still hope to do *very* well materially (although they have some sense that the tide of certain material success may be going out, requiring them to work a little harder and be a little shrewder). While as a generation they are described as having more awareness of social responsibility than those just ahead of them,[50] they expect this social responsibility to be fulfilled through philanthropy and volunteerism rather than by means of significant changes in either the system or their personal lifestyles. What present MBA students most share with their younger brothers and sisters is the concern for "balance"—an abiding hope that they will not have to achieve their career success at the price of their personal lives.[51]

Success and Balance

We assumed that for these young adults "success" would be a salient category of value, and indeed it was. What surprised us was that, when discussing the forms of success to which they aspire, the majority of the students (and even more men than women) explicitly mentioned a desire for balance as well as success. For example, when asked, "What is your sense of what constitutes success?" one student responded, "I think it's balance. I think it's having a very successful business life and means being successful in what you do without sacrificing everything else, friends and family, leisure and life outside of work." As in this example, balance typically meant a desire for equilibrium between values marking career success (such as a stimulating job, job status, money, visibility, power, and challenging, creative responsibility) on the one hand, and values signifying a quality of personal life (such as affection, marriage, family, time for leisure and/or sports-fitness activities, the arts, travel, vacations, and interaction with nature) on the other. (A small number of students included in the latter domain desires "some kind of influence on some little corner of the world," to "make a social contribution that is more than checks," and to "expand [my] voice outside the office in the community.") The desire for balance was strong; confidence that it could be achieved was somewhat ambiguous. Several students expressed a willingness to sacrifice balance in the immediate few years in the hope that they might have it later. It is notable that the one form of failure these students as a group seemed to have some capacity to acknowledge was the failure to achieve balance.

If this student generation is to critique and modify the conditions of the world in which it is coming into adulthood, doubt must somewhere be their ally. Their marked yearning for balance seems to be the strongest lever of doubt in relationship to the conventional ethos in which these young adults dwell and aspire. Primary factors that give rise to this doubt

seem to be that they have seen (and in many cases have been a
part of) family sacrifices that they do not choose to repeat.
Others have observed burnout (and early heart attacks) in their
parents or bosses. Some watched the lives of colleagues sink
into meaninglessness after the stock market crash of 1987. (It
may also be that company takeovers and the like have muted
their expectation that they are working for anything more
than themselves anyway.) These students want the same success as the previous generation and are willing to work hard
for it, but they hope to achieve it on different terms.

The yearning for balance is a primary, natural pathway into
critical thought and ethical reflection for this generation of
young adults. It is here that they are most personally ready
to declare that "something isn't right—maybe we could do it
better." [52]

The Exceptions

A Critical and Constructive Stance

Although no student precisely fits the general description outlined thus far—each one, in fact, diverging in some manner
from this profile—a few represented significant exceptions.
These exceptions warrant attention, for they appear to embody the promise of a more critical and comprehensive stance
toward both self and world. For example, although most responded to our question about who they might hurt with the
hope that they would not hurt anyone, a few responses were
dramatically different from the more interpersonal responses
described earlier. One student who hoped to go into consulting remarked that it was her experience that "when you go in
to shape up a company, you inevitably hurt the production
people . . . [and] it is, therefore, important to have good compensation packages" (which she believed the company she had
worked for had in place). Another student, who expected to
continue to work with a major chemical corporation, responded: "As long as I stay in chemicals, for my generation
and for my children's generation, we will probably hurt the

environment; but I think I can make a difference in how much we do that."

There were other students who also seemed able to take both a critical, systemic (and typically also constructive) stance outside prevailing assumptions. These students who were exceptions seemed to have certain characteristics: they either belonged to an ethnic minority, were female, were from the military, and/or had had a significant encounter with "otherness." Some had dealt with life-and-death situations. Some were slightly older than the average age of twenty-six. All had somehow broken out of conventional forms of socioeconomic isolation. That is to say, although these students whom we identify as exceptions were as successful as the rest of their peers in the program, they were no longer as subject to the unreflective conditions of the "flow of success." In the interviews they consistently demonstrated the capacity to exercise critical thought in relationship to self and world. They were able to make meaning in more complex and systemic forms. Their faith could tolerate greater ambiguity, and they were less subject to the authority of assumed conventions. They also seemed to feel somehow different from the majority of students in the program; and although very much involved in the broad range of activities of the school, they felt a certain minority status even if they were not part of a recognized minority group. This often meant, they reported, that they were slow to say what they really thought in discussions both inside and outside of class. This seemed to bespeak not so much a lack of courage but a realistic perception of the power of the norms in the environment and what, therefore, could be heard and understood.

Most of the students we identify as exceptions seem to have had good mentors of whom they were somewhat prematurely bereft. Now located in a totally new environment, they are vulnerable, especially initially, to the appearance of merely conforming to the norms of those who reflect in less complex forms than they. If the learning environment does not offer an ongoing challenge to their emerging strength—that is, their capacity to critically engage the ethical challenges of business management so as to provide the potential leadership that they represent, they may be vulnerable over time to stasis, to merely a holding action.

It is interesting that the students we describe as exceptions were somewhat less enthusiastic than were their peers about the ethics module, apparently because they had already been initiated into critical reflection on complexity and ambiguity and were ready for further challenge.

The Other Exceptions

We suspect that there is another group of students who also are exceptions to the general profile we have presented, among them the very few who declined to be interviewed, or who more typically "didn't have the time" to respond to our request. These are the few, perhaps "crass," students whom other students describe as a small but real minority. They are perceived to be more or less ruthless in their commitments to self and material success. These students also represent some of the complexity and ambiguity the typical entering student encounters. The conventional student who comes to the MBA program assuming a certain degree of goodwill in others is sometimes a bit astonished at what a few classmates are willing to articulate and practice. As one student expressed it, "I never knew before that someone's 'ethics' could be immoral." Such encounters, which are an inevitable feature of ongoing experience in society, provide occasion for new depths of reflection upon self and world. If such occasions are not to end in mere relativism, they need to be recognized as an opportunity and challenge to the faculty and curricula of professional schools.

Moral Courage

Any approach to teaching ethics in relation to managerial leadership and decision making must recognize that it is not difficult to teach moral philosophy or ethical systems theory to the bright, talented young adults we have described here. The more sobering and challenging task is to develop a curriculum that fosters not only ethical reflection but also the formation of moral courage.[53] The age-old conundrum of knowing one thing and doing another does not constitute ethical competence. The only question that finally matters is this: Have young adults preparing for careers in business management been enabled *to act* in ways that are not only legal, but just; not only defensible, but compassionate; not only efficient, but consistent with a moral vision that adequately embraces the complex and interdependent claims of contemporary life?

Meaning and Mentors

To foster moral courage—the capacity not only to know the good, but also to act—requires attention to the ground of action, the meaning-making of young adults that includes both intellect and feelings, both reason and social formation. As described earlier, a young adult, like other human beings, will act in a manner that is consistent with his or her ultimate meaning system—what is understood in the head, heart, and gut to be the way things really are. But young adulthood is unique in the form of its readiness to reflect critically upon self and world, and to recompose more fitting meanings and understandings by which to live. As the young adult engages these tasks, he or she manifests a unique combination of power and vulnerability: on the one hand a new readiness for adult responsibility, and on the other a yet appropriate dependence upon mentoring authority.

Mentoring Forms of Authority

Primary attention must thus be given to the young adult's orientation to authority. The conventionally reflective but uncritical young adult finally will trust authority outside the self in an essentially unexamined, unquestioned fashion (see Appendix). This does not necessarily mean blind obedience to a dictator; more typically, it means reflective but uncritical participation in assumed patterns and conventions. This form of thinking is characteristic of many students when they first come to us, but they are ready for more.

In contrast, the person who is fully young adult thinks in a more critical fashion; he or she is not only able to engage in reflective thought within a given set of conditions, but also able to step outside prevailing conditions and assumptions in the figurative sense and consider the sources of the conditions—why and how things have come to be the way they are. The students we observed are fully capable of this kind of thought; what they need is the leadership and environments that support it. Leadership is particularly crucial for the young adult still appropriately dependent upon authority outside the self, because a key shift can occur at this juncture—a shift from external authority that is merely assumed to authority that is chosen. It is facilitated by an allegiance (or better, attraction) prompted by a resonance between the young adult's emerging, more critically considered experience and the perspective offered by a mentoring form of authority. Young adults are thus *appropriately dependent* upon the mentors who are available in their environment (see Appendix). Mentoring does not require lecturing, nor, as will be discussed later, does it necessarily assume a one-to-one relationship. A mentor's function is to recognize and affirm the emerging competence of the young adult, while beckoning forth the promise of the young adult life and making accessible a viable and desirable pathway into the future.[54] In so doing, mentors honor the young adult's new power to critique the world as it is, and readiness to envision both world and self as they might become.

A Mentor Is Not Enough

The business sector has exhibited greater sophistication than most other sectors in recognizing the significance of the mentoring function in career development.[55] Indeed, for a young adult about to be initiated into the corporation and/or the society as presently constituted, the contribution of a good mentor can be both strategic and sufficient. But growing evidence suggests that for the young adult to participate in the corporation and the society, not as they are, but as they might become, not only a mentor but a *mentoring community* is required.[56] A mentoring community is a group (which could take the form of a class, a task force or working group, or even a corporation or a division of a corporation) that welcomes and affirms the competence and promise of young adult lives, while offering a vision on behalf of a larger possibility and an experience of acting together in concert with that vision.

It appears that the young adults who must enter and help to shape an unprecedented future need more than individual mentors or sponsors; they also need the confidence that there is and will be a "we." All human beings, even the bold and daring, need to belong. The young adult, in particular, needs to know that if he or she is going to challenge the norms of prevailing conventions on behalf of a more adequate business competitiveness guided by a more profound ethical imagination, he or she will not be alone in that effort. A generation that must necessarily challenge prevailing conditions will thus require both mentors and mentoring communities.

The present generation cannot merely be initiated into the world as it is, because the world—and certainly the world of business—is changing dramatically. The rise of a global economy and global markets, the emergence of a more highly educated and international work force, ever-growing dependence upon sophisticated technologies, the increasing need for collaborative decision making, heightened ecological awareness, the growing presence of women and minorities in the workplace, and the expanded role of business institutions within society—all conspire to create new managerial challenges and confound former ethical assumptions. This generation will not be able to play by the old rules. It confronts a set of conditions that calls for the reconsideration of values, purpose, and vision. This generation stands on a new ethical frontier and faces the task of composing meaning in new forms.[57]

It is for these reasons that young adults of this generation require both mentors and mentoring communities with whom they can critically reflect upon things as they now are and chart a viable course toward how they might be in the coming millennium. Renewed interest in business ethics is not simply a reaction to the scandals and abuses of the 1980s, nor is it merely the manifestation of a simple hope that we can return to a former civility. The present historical context places everyone on a new ethical frontier, and the call for renewed attention to ethics in managerial decision making arises from an increasingly shared intuition that a new and more complex ethical frame is emerging that demands the generation of more adequate wisdom. History always gives this task to young adults and their mentors.[58]

Implications for the Teaching of Ethics

Movement to Critical-Systemic Thought

In light of all that has been suggested and described here, one of the first concerns of a curriculum that will foster ongoing ethical development is the cultivation of critical-systemic thought (see Chapter Four). Students become more critically aware when they are invited to recognize competing authorities and claims, thereby stepping outside of tacit assumptions. Our interviews provide clear evidence that student thinking becomes more critical and open when interpersonal modes of morality are played out against larger systems of multifaceted and competing claims—claims, in other words, that thwart any attempt to measure "the good" in terms of a single individual or action. The intention here is not to render interpersonal morality irrelevant, but to bring it into a wider frame of discourse and judgment in which the interpersonal and the systemic can be held in creative and responsible tension.

Tolerance of Complexity in the Service of a New Imagination

Embedded in the move to systemic thought is the cultivation of the ability to tolerate complexity and ambiguity in the service of composing new frames of meaning—in essence, a new imagination. Some so-called ethical thought that is unnecessarily naive is maintained because individuals in isolation "can handle only so much." This is one of those instances in which consciousness of a "we"—a mentoring community—becomes crucial: when the multifaceted ethical dimensions of managerial decision making begin to be recognized and engaged by an entire class of students, the complexity that cannot be tolerated by an individual can be accommodated by the whole. And this means that reality, even with its infinite complexity, has a better chance of carrying the day. To be sure, every group has investments in various distortions of reality; but a dialectic of perspectives is the best insurance against the formation of an ethic that is too partial to be practical.

Cultivation of Diverse Perspectives

An integral part of the development of a more broadly informed and complex perspective is the cultivation of diverse points of view. Fostering diversity of perspective in the curriculum serves two dimensions of ethical formation. First, the complexity (and therefore the reality) is heightened. Second, a more empathic imagination is fostered. Studies of those who have exercised moral courage indicate that such people have the capacity to take the perspectives of others, to "walk in another's moccasins" and thereby practice an empathic imagination.[59] A capacity for empathy (as opposed to pity) is the ground of compassion—the ability to suffer *with*—and the driving energy in the formation of the ethical imagination. By "empathy" we do not mean the sentimental or romantic, or practices best consigned to therapists. Rather, we interpret empathy as a strength manifested in the ability to see things from multiple perspectives, be affected by them, and take them into account. The capacity for empathy is a primary element in the formation of effective, ethical managerial behavior.

An empathic imagination is cultivated by introducing cases and problems that place important, compelling points of view in tension with each other. This is facilitated, in part, by fostering a diverse population in the classroom, which affords students the opportunity to bring differing contexts of experience and competence to bear on the discussion. Thus "curriculum development" that is sensitive to education in ethics must be defined broadly enough to include admissions policies as well as course structure and content.

We already have evidence that a more diverse classroom fosters an awareness that would hardly have been possible in the not-too-distant past, when the typical MBA classroom was populated almost exclusively by white, young adult males from homogeneous backgrounds. Indeed, our interviews revealed that some diversity—notably the presence of women—has become, at least in some cases, part of the conventional experience of business and classroom culture. That is to say, some degree of pluralism has replaced homogeneity as the conventional ethos, but only to a point.

In many instances our interviews revealed only a rudimentary awareness of the differing perspectives women bring to the business culture, and there was a markedly lower awareness of the experience and perspectives of ethnic and other cultural minorities—both national and international. This was particularly notable among those who are most comfortable and successful within the norms of the conventionally presumed environment. Consider the following exchange in the second interview.

INTERVIEWER: "It has been remarked that racism is more apt to take subtle rather than more overt forms in this environment; what is your perception of that?"

STUDENT (A WHITE, TWENTY-SEVEN-YEAR-OLD MALE): "I would say were I to perceive that it existed, I'm certain that it would take a subtle form because the norms of the larger group are not accepting of that kind of behavior."

INTERVIEWER: "But you don't perceive it as existing?"

STUDENT: "I don't perceive it as existing."

Other students observed that although they do not see subtle forms of racism in the environment, they have become aware that Afro-American students apparently do see patterns of subtle discrimination. In contrast, the students who, in our sample, constitute "exceptions" readily recognized subtle but real forms of discrimination in the conventional ethos.[60]

Ethics: Integral to the Entire Curriculum

Because the conventional ethos of this society presumes a split between commerce and values, it is essential that the business curriculum be designed so that ethics cannot be perceived as "a matter set apart." Given the cultural milieu in which most of them dwell, many students arrive with the mind-set articulated by one student who advised his classmates that they should do business during the week and "wait to save the whales on the weekend." This young man is yet unaware of the number of business decisions made every day that directly affect not only the whales, but all that he intended "the whales" to symbolize. His comment alerts us to the educationally strategic importance of recognizing that, since every managerial decision—large or small, at all levels of the organization—has embedded within it multiple ethical choices that often reach well beyond the boundaries of the corporation itself, the capacity to recognize and articulate the ethical scope of every managerial decision needs to be cultivated as a skill integral to responsible and professional managerial practice. Western culture's artificial ruptures between commerce, the rest of society, and values can be addressed in part by legitimizing ethical discourse within business practice and fostering shared language and norms by which such discourse can occur within and across all functional areas.

Both the What and the How

Ethical choices in business involve not only the "how," but also the "what." *How* something is to be marketed may be fraught with any number of moral questions, but *what* is to be marketed may be a moral question as well. When asked, "What goods and services do you think are needed at this time in our society (defined either in national or global terms)?" many students revealed that this was not a question they had previously considered, and their responses were surprisingly vague. Said one, "We probably need more technology"; another, "We need more health care." A third responded, after a pause, "Is education a service?"

The objective of the business professional is frequently defined simply in terms of securing a position with a company—a "good company." But a good company is most apt to be defined by its general working conditions, profitability, and status; its product, except in extreme cases, is not likely to be reflected upon in moral terms.[61] Similarly, for students who aspire to the management of their own company, the nature of the product or service seemed to be of only minor significance. Most graduate and professional schools are inclined to focus on formal categories to the neglect of the contents within those forms. Yet a good deal is at stake in whether the business academy will search out appropriate ways of inviting students, both collectively and as individuals, to contend with this fundamental set of questions as an integral part of ethical competence in business decision making.[62]

"Balance" as a Pathway to Critical Reflection

As noted earlier, the theme of "balance"—that is, the concern for a balanced life—is an area of striking consensus among the students we interviewed. Although typically construed in limited interpersonal terms (e.g., a desire for quality family life and/or time for vacations), balance may well be the most lively and resonant starting place for a discussion that opens the door to broader, systemic ethical issues. After students have been initiated into ethics as a systemic rather than a merely personal or interpersonal matter, introducing the issue of balance engages this generation of students at the place where they are personally most invested, readiest to critique "business as usual," and best able to recognize a pathway into the systemic issues of social responsibility. This pathway can lead these young adults toward places where they can make connections between their own yearnings for balance and broader organizational and social policy—for example, into the issues of women in the work force and ecological responsibility, which are the two broad systemic issues that make some substantial claim on this generation. But however it arises and wherever it leads, the issue of balance appears to be the primary crack in the imaginative edifice of the contemporary MBA student— an imagination that is often conventionally constrained but promisingly fertile.

Rigorous Analysis and Informed Imagination

It is vital to recognize that education in ethics has not occurred if students are initiated only into complexity and ambiguity. These can become mere stepping stones to the moral relativism so decried by Allan Bloom and other critics of our educational institutions.[63] Neither can students, no matter how much respect we have for their talent and commitment, merely be entrusted with (or abandoned to) deciding for themselves what they want to do. Young adults, being appropriately dependent upon the mentors, strategies, and visions accessible in their environment, must not only be given access to tools and models for rigorous analysis, but must also be inspired and empowered to imagine solutions, some of which may be reclaimed from ancient wisdoms, some as yet untried. This requires attention to both the teaching process in the classroom and the content of the curriculum.

Classroom Process

Cultivating a Sense of Moral Agency

Studies of individuals who have manifested the capacity to exercise moral courage suggest that such persons have learned the art of "previewing for a purposeful life"; that is, they have learned to anticipate and reflect upon their possible behavior in heretofore unexperienced situations. They are proactive (as opposed to reactive) and prosocial (as opposed to antisocial).[64] Students who seek careers in business management, and certainly those who are admitted to the most outstanding business schools, are typically highly prosocial (outgoing, extroverted) and thus predisposed toward at least some forms of social engagement. But many of these same students also tend to be reactive (passive respondents in the flow of success) rather than proactive. Consequently, they may be less active than we might expect in anticipating and cultivating the full range of choices and behaviors available to them and, in reference to ethics, in planning to act in ways that have a positive and beneficial impact on the lives and circumstances of both themselves and others.

This set of observations suggests two things. First, these students need to be given opportunities for active, critical reflection upon the circumstances and opportunities before them. Second, they must be encouraged to become more active agents, most immediately in the present context of their own educational process.

Alas, across all disciplines, most graduate school programs foster some measure of infantilization. Often unwittingly, they encourage adult students to function as something less than the adults they are. Most encourage some degree of passivity—a presumed dependence upon the wisdom of the faculty and the value of the program. As we have implied earlier, however, a professional curriculum that strives to be ethically committed discourages such passivity. Instead it promotes responsibility, choice, authentic competition, inner dependence, active collaboration, and respectful, meaningful evaluation. It disallows in the immediate environment the convenient student perception that matters of real ethical significance are taken care of by someone else in the organization. In presenting such a curriculum, the educational institution fosters a habit of mind and being that the young adult is ready to inculcate and transfer to other environments. (Failure to foster this sort of personal agency arrests a young adult in a passive, dependent mode of being, just as he or she is in a primary period of adult formation.)

This dimension of ethical education—the capacity to be proactive—is significant for any given individual, but it is notably enhanced when a *group* of young adult students discovers a shared power to imagine and to make ethical judgments in complex circumstances so as to foster a greater good than could have been achieved by one individual. Research still in process suggests that those who later in life demonstrate significant leadership in matters of ethics and social responsibility were, in their young adulthood, typically a part of a group—a "we," a mentoring community—that shared a vision and practice that effected significant and meaningful systemic change. Although direct affiliation with this group is not usually sustained, it appears that the experience is carried internally, forming a conviction of possibility that empowers future commitment and action.

If this is so, then we must regard every classroom as a potential "we" that can achieve something of significance. If, for example, a class can create a critically considered set of norms of positive group conduct and purpose, each individual within that class stands to gain confidence in his or her capacity to provide ethical leadership for an organization, not only in interpersonal modes, but also in the creation and implementation of systemic norms of policy and practice. This sort of experience within a rigorous educational context can also serve as a powerful antidote to the cynicism that marks our collective life, particularly among the young.[65]

Encouraging Student Leadership

The sorts of goals outlined here are achieved in part by encouraging the voice of the more mature students in the class. What we mean here by "more mature" is exemplified in the students identified as exceptions in our sample. Those students are critical thinkers, prepared to contend with complexity and ambiguity and to constructively challenge more naive forms of ethical engagement. People tend to be attracted to the places slightly ahead of where they are in their own ethical development. Thus, if students who offer a more complex question, conviction, or imagination are not marginalized but instead are brought into the mainstream of discourse, other students will follow. But it must be underscored that when the majority of the students are context driven, they will be unlikely to respond initially to what these students offer, unless the context encourages them to do so, which brings us to the strategic role of the faculty.

Faculty: Key Figures in Shaping Mentoring Environments

A faculty member facing from twenty to ninety bright, talented young adults may wonder how much power and authority he or she really has as a professor and teacher. Indeed, even the more passive, context-driven students may be ruthless in their expectations that authority figures fit assumed norms and conventions. The more critically thinking young adults in the class will likewise appear formidable, giving credence only to authorities who make sense to them in terms of their own experience.

Nevertheless, the potential power of faculty in young adult lives cannot be overstated. As discussed earlier, even critically aware young adults remain appropriately dependent upon authority external to the self. Kenneth Keniston was the first to recognize young adulthood as a new, post-adolescent period in the life span.[66] Re-examining what had earlier been described in such pejorative terms as "prolonged adolescence," Keniston recognized a new stage in human becoming—a stage shaped by the extended educational preparation required for competence in a more complex society, the extension of life expectancy, and a wider array of career and lifestyle options. In the past, achieving a critically aware identity and a place in adult society could be accomplished as the single task of adolescence. Now it appears that for many, and specifically for those we studied, these are two separate tasks. Becoming a critically aware self—that is, achieving a sense of separate identity—marks the completion of adolescence. Finding a fitting place for that self in adult society (or better, finding the fitting relationship between self and society) is an additional and very complex task. This task is the hallmark of young adulthood.

Thus the critically aware young adult, although very capable of critiquing both self and society, must necessarily pass through a time of "the wary probe"—exploring and testing the strengths of both self and society in a critical reimagining of self and world. As elaborated earlier, during this period young adults remain appropriately dependent upon authority external to the self (though only authorities, images, and values that make sense in terms of the young adult's own experience will have formative power). As a consequence, young adults are vulnerable to and limited by whatever images of self and society as are accessible in their environment; these images and the values they convey are mediated by mentors and mentoring environments (see Appendix).

Any conventional environment will serve a quasi-mentoring function for the uncritical young adult. That is to say, the media and other shapers of conventional sociocultural norms have decisive influence and power. It was striking, for example, when asked where they gleaned their images of business, how many students who did not come from business families mentioned (without prompting) television or other media as a significant source of their image of business management. Such images orient the assumptions and norms toward which the MBA student may uncritically direct her or his ambitions and aspirations. These images, either reinforced or modified when the young adult enters an actual business environment, retain power until there is occasion for critical reflection upon them. A mentoring environment will encourage such critical thought.

The Professor as Mentor

Critically thinking young adults, although they may bring to the MBA classroom a very mixed set of thoughtful affirmations and critiques of conventional business practice, remain appropriately dependent in certain respects. They are dependent not upon assumed, conventional, or arbitrary authority, but upon mentoring, guiding authority who can help them forge a viable perspective and competence upon which their contributions to the business world will rest. To function effectively for the critically aware young adult, authority—professorial or otherwise—must function in a mentoring mode. Effective faculty mentors do not make pronouncements from on high, for there is no blind acceptance of authority (even if held in high repute) among these students. Rather, they are able to make sense to the students in terms of the students' own experiences. Moreover, mentors must possess the grace and strength to convey enormous respect for the emerging competence of the young adult, while simultaneously serving as a beacon that offers a compelling sense of direction in a complex and perilous world.

The mentoring professor will be watched by the young adult student as a person with a style, commitments, and a track record of failures and successes, all conveyed primarily in implicit forms. It was clear in the responses of the students we interviewed, for example, that the ethics module at HBS was effective for them in significant measure because they respected the seasoned, informed faculty who led it, finding them credible as individuals. This credibility is revealed in part through the classroom process—the manner in which professors respond to students, who and what receives a positive response, attitudes toward risk and failure, how much diversity is respected, what degree of complexity is tolerated, and what norms of discourse (including forms of humor) are allowed or discouraged.[67]

When our focus is the ethically committed curriculum, we must also recognize that just as a young adult can be mentored into a positive practice of social responsibility, a young adult also can be mentored into the Mafia. The educational environment committed to ethical formation must be attentive to both the dynamic form of the professor/mentor-student relationship and the *content,* both explicit and implicit, that is mediated thereby.

Mentoring professors, therefore, do not only embody and thus teach matters of style and attitude. They also exercise enormous power in their choice of explicit curricular content—the issues, concepts, strategies, skills, forms of analysis, and visions of the future they choose to make accessible to students. Included in the choice of content will be other persons made available as additional mentoring figures, either through personal encounters or media presentations. Such choices of content exert great power in the ongoing meaning-making of the young adult. What a mentoring professor includes will constitute primary sources for the young adult imagination; what the mentoring professor excludes will be neglected in the young adult imagination.

In light of the individualism and insulation so endemic to this generation, part of the content ethically sensitive mentors need to make available are images of interdependence, collaboration, and cooperation that enhance competitiveness as a positive outcome in the business culture. Such an effort will challenge the mind-set of many in this generation, while simultaneously encouraging responsible creativity in addressing some of the central and most confounding problems for which they must develop strategies and solutions, including a new power to contribute to the common good through competent business practice.[68]

The Power to Create Mentoring Environments

Clearly, given the full range of issues that ethics embraces in managerial preparation and practice, the young adult is best served by a team of mentors who collectively accept responsibility for the character and quality of the mentoring environment they inevitably mediate. This recognition invites faculty and administrators to self-consciously cultivate the strength of a mentoring educational environment in which multiple mentoring voices mutually enhance and inform the young adult imagination. Thus the business-educational institution that recognizes its inevitable influence in the ethical formation of young adults will examine every facet of its operation so as to be accountable as a primary shaper of the patterns of managerial discourse and practice young adults will experience as the stuff of their meaning-making and consequent actions, as they make their way into full adulthood with its multifaceted opportunities and responsibilities.

Fostering a Competent and Confident Faculty

Because faculty are the primary shapers and mediators of the educational curriculum, both implicit and explicit, administrative leadership concerned with the ethical influence of the educational institution upon students will invest appropriate resources in the recruitment and support of faculty, with particular attention being paid to the creation of a corporate culture in which the ethical dimensions of the curriculum are enunciated and effectively nurtured. This includes a conscious effort to cultivate in the faculty both confidence and competence in the teaching of ethics and social responsibility. Because most faculty have been formed in institutions that reflect the traditional dichotomies between commerce and values and between theory and practice, and because a significant percentage of faculty are themselves yet young adults, this challenge dwells at the core of the commitment to readdress ethics in the business curriculum (see Chapter Three). We have found this a challenge to which most business faculty—those who have chosen vocations in both education and commerce—are prepared to respond with a critical, informed, and competent imagination.

Appendix

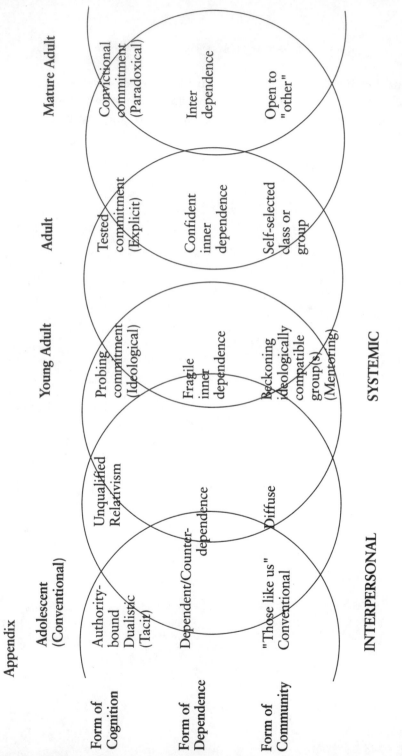

	Adolescent (Conventional)		Young Adult		Adult		Mature Adult
Form of Cognition	Authority-bound Dualistic (Tacit)	Unqualified Relativism	Probing commitment (Ideological)		Tested commitment (Explicit)		Convictional commitment (Paradoxical)
Form of Dependence	Dependent/Counter-dependence		Fragile inner dependence		Confident inner dependence		Inter dependence
Form of Community	"Those like us" Conventional	Diffuse	Beckoning ideologically compatible group(s) (Mentoring)		Self-selected class or group		Open to "other"
		INTERPERSONAL		**SYSTEMIC**			

Source: Adapted from a table in *The Critical Years* by Sharon Parks (San Francisco: Harper Collins, 1986).

NOTES

1. E. J. Conry and D. R. Nelson, "Business Law and Moral Growth," *American Business Law Journal* 27 (1989) pp. 1–39; Jeffrey Gandz and Nadine Hayes, "Teaching Business Ethics," *Journal of Business Ethics* 7 (1988) pp. 657–669; James Rest, "Can Ethics Be Taught In Professional Schools? The Psychological Research," *Easier Said Than Done* (Winter 1988), pp. 22–26; James Rest et al., *Moral Development: Advances in Research and Theory* (Westport, CT: Praeger, 1986); Muriel J. Bebeau, "Can Ethics Be Taught? A Look at the Evidence," *Practicing Dentist* (Spring 1991), pp. 5, 10–15.

2. Rest, "Can Ethics Be Taught in Professional Schools?," p. 22; Bebeau, "Can Ethics Be Taught? A Look at the Evidence," p. 13.

3. Martha Nussbaum, "Aristophanes and Socrates on Learning Practical Wisdom," in Jeffrey Henderson, ed., *Yale Classical Studies* 26 (Cambridge: Cambridge University Press, 1980) pp. 43–97, quoted by Stanley Hawerwas, "How Christian Universities Contribute to the Corruption of Youth: Church and University in a Confused Age," *Katallagete*, p. 25.

4. Rest, "Can Ethics Be Taught in Professional Schools?," p. 25.

5. James R. Rest, "Moral Judgment: An Interesting Variable for Higher Education Research," paper for the Annual Convention of the Association for the Study of Higher Education, Baltimore, MD, November 21, 1987.

6. Thomas M. Jones, "Can Business Ethics Be Taught? Empirical Evidence," *Business and Professional Ethics Journal,* vol. 8, no. 2, p. 84.

7. Traditionally, as with any of the professions, the justification of business was rooted firmly in the public good. The ancient understanding of economy was rooted in the notion of livelihood for all. This was significantly modified but not totally obscured with the rise of market capitalism and concomitant presumption that the self-interested pursuit of competitive profit would result in the good community. The increasing erosion of this faith and the absence of a compelling alternative leaves the pursuit of personal profit without an anchoring and broader purpose.

8. William G. Bowen and Julie A. Sosa, *Prospects for Faculty in the Arts and Sciences: A Study of Factors Affecting Demand and Supply* (Princeton: Princeton University Press, 1989), p. 48.

9. Willis W. Harman, "For A New Society, A New Economics, World Good Will," The United Nations Division for Economic and Social Information, *Development Forum* XV, 3–5 (1987), p. 10.

10. Leroy S. Rouner, in R. Dickie and L. Rouner, eds., *Corporations and the Common Good* (Notre Dame, IN: University of Notre Dame Press, 1986), p. vii.

11. See Kenneth R. Andrews, *Ethics in Practice: Managing the Moral Corporation* (Boston: Harvard Business School Press, 1989), Introduction, pp. 2–6.

12. Amitai Etzioni, *Business and Society Review* (Summer 1989), pp. 18–19.

13. A second interviewer from outside the school interviewed five of the students. This was necessitated by the time frame but also contributed to the analysis.

14. See Sharon Parks, *The Critical Years: Young Adults and the Search for Meaning, Faith, and Commitment* (San Francisco: Harper Collins, 1986).

15. See Parks, *The Critical Years,* Chapter 2.

16. See Robert Kegan, *The Evolving Self: Meaning and Process in Human Development* (Cambridge, MA: Harvard University Press, 1981); James W. Fowler, *Stages of Faith: The Psychology of Human Development and the Quest for Meaning* (San Francisco: Harper & Row, 1982); Parks, *The Critical Years,* Chapter 2; William G. Perry, *Intellectual and Ethical Development in the College Years* (New York: Holt, 1968).

17. See Meryl Reis Louis, "Acculturation in the Workplace: Newcomers as Lay Ethnographers," in B. Schneider, ed., *Organizational Climate and Culture* (San Francisco: Jossey-Bass, 1990).

18. See Parks, *The Critical Years,* Chapter 4.

19. Ibid., Chapter 5.

20. A subsequent study of international students is in progress.

21. Prof. Kenneth Goodpaster has helpfully identified this set of conditions as "teleopathy." See Kenneth E. Goodpaster, "Ethical Imperative and Corporate Leadership," in Andrews, *Ethics in Practice,* pp. 217–218.

22. See Fowler, *Stages of Faith,* pp. 276–281.

23. Michael Josephson observes the tendency to self-protection and self-righteousness—the desire to avoid unpleasant and embar-

rassing confrontation and the tendency to judge ourselves in terms of our best and most noble virtues and motivations. "Teaching Ethical Decision Making and Principled Reasoning," *Ethics: Easier Said Than Done,* 1 (1988), pp. 27–33, quoted in Bebeau, "Can Ethics Be Taught? A Look at the Evidence," p. 10.

24. For this interpretation the author is indebted in part to Dr. Patricia K. Light, director and chief psychologist of MBA Counseling Services, Harvard Business School.

25. For the concept "ethic of control," I am indebted to Sharon D. Welch, *A Feminist Ethic of Risk* (Minneapolis. Fortress Press, 1990), Chapter 2.

26. Abraham Zaleznik, *The Managerial Mystique: Restoring Leadership in Business* (New York: Harper & Row, 1989), pp. 4–5.

27. See R. Edward Freeman and Daniel R. Gilbert, "Business, Ethics, and Society: A Critical Agenda" unpublished paper, Darden School of Business Administration, University of Virginia, 1991.

28. See Parks, *The Critical Years,* esp. Chapters 6 and 7.

29. Albert Z. Carr, "Is Business Bluffing Ethical?" in Andrews, *Ethics in Practice,* pp. 99–109; and John J. Clancy, *The Invisible Powers: The Language of Business* (Lexington, MA: Lexington Books, 1989), Chapter 5.

30. See Leonard Greenhalgh and Deborah I. Chapman, "Relationships and Conflict: A Model and Typology," paper submitted for review for the Power, Negotiation, and Conflict Management Interest Group program, Academy of Management Annual Meeting, San Francisco, August 1990; and Leonard Greenhalgh, "Strategic Choice In Conflicts: The Importance of Relationships," in R. Kahn and M. Zald, eds., *Nations and Organizations* (San Francisco: Jossey-Bass, 1990), and "The Case Against Winning in Negotiations," *Negotiation Journal* (April 1987), pp. 167–173.

31. See Howard H. Stevenson, "Is Business a Game of Poker?" presentation slides for Decision Making and Ethical Values, Harvard Business School, September 17, 1991.

32. Donald L. Kanter and Phillip H. Mirvis, *The Cynical Americans: Living and Working in an Age of Discontent and Disillusion* (San Francisco: Jossey-Bass, 1989).

33. Arthur Levine, *When Dreams and Heroes Died: A Portrait of Today's College Student* (San Francisco: Jossey-Bass, 1980).

34. Ibid., p. 113. It can be speculated that the pursuit of physical fit-

ness as discussed earlier may be fueled in some measure by this desire to build an island of personal security in the face of a nagging fear of disempowerment—a physical response to being overwhelmed. Corporations likewise may pursue fitness by getting bigger (more muscular) and "lean and mean" in order to survive. This is resonant with an ethic predicated exclusively on the values of competition and control with winners and losers narrowly conceived, in contrast to a more interdependent conception balancing competition and cooperation.

35. See D. C. Denison, "The Interview: Arthur Schlesinger," *Boston Globe Magazine,* November 29, 1987, p. 2; and Michael Oreskes, "A Trait of Today's Youth: Apathy to Public Affairs," *New York Times,* June 28, 1990, citing studies from the Times Mirror Center for the People and the Press (1990); and Peter D. Hart, "Democracy's Next Generation," People for the American Way, 1989.

36. See Thomas Berry, *The Dream of the Earth* (San Francisco: Sierra Club Books, 1988).

37. See Charles Kenney and Robert L. Turner, "A Generation Adrift: The Post-Vietnam Generation's Search for Identity," *Boston Globe Magazine,* September 3, 1989, pp. 16–19ff.

38. Professor Quinn Mills in faculty consultation.

39. Robert Reich, *The Work of Nations: Preparing Ourselves for 21st Century Capitalism* (New York: Alfred A. Knopf, 1991).

40. See Robert Bellah et al., *Habits of the Heart* (Berkeley: University of California Press, 1985); and Reich, *The Work of Nations.*

41. "At present, Americans are the most parochial of all industrial peoples. Young people in America are less likely to travel abroad, less likely to speak a foreign language, and less likely to know the basics of world history or geography than their counterparts in any other advanced nation. This parochialism already costs us daily in international competition and international affairs and leaves us ill-prepared for the future." Derek Bok, Harvard Commencement Address, June 7, 1990, *Harvard Alumni Gazette* (June 1990), p. 25.

42. See Richard R. Niebuhr, "The Tragic Play of Symbols," *Harvard Theological Review* 75, 1 (1982), pp. 32–33.

43. Suzi Gablik, in Milenko Matanovic, ed., *Lightworks* (Issaquah, WA: Lorian Press, 1985), p. 10.

44. See George C. Lodge, *The New American Ideology* (New York:

Alfred A. Knopf, 1976); and *Perestroika for America* (Boston: Harvard Business School Press, 1990).

45. Note the psychological dynamics that can be fostered by this set of conditions, particularly "splitting" and "doubling." See Robert J. Lifton, *The Nazi Doctors: Medical Killing and the Psychology of Genocide* (New York: Basic Books, 1986), Chapter 19.

46. ". . . religion is less help than it once might have been when membership in a distinct community promoted . . . conventional moral behavior. . . . Nor does higher education take up the slack." Kenneth R. Andrews, "Ethics in Practice," *Harvard Business Review* (September–October, 1989), p. 102.

47. John Kotter, "Leadership as Social Capital: An Agenda for the Future," *Power and Influence* (New York: Free Press), Chapter 11.

48. See D. Quinn Mills, *Not Like Our Parents: A New Look at How the Baby Boom Generation is Changing America* (New York: William Morrow, 1987).

49. See "Twentysomething: Proceeding with Caution," *Time,* July 16, 1990, pp. 57–62. See also "What Lies Ahead: Countdown to the 21st Century," United Way of America, Alexandria, VA, 1989.

50. This is particularly evident in renewed attention to volunteerism.

51. See also "The 25 Year-Olds: Today's Young Managers Are Nothing Like Yuppies," *Fortune,* August 27, 1990, pp. 42–50.

52. While students speak of balance as a personal or interpersonal challenge, note the systemic nature of these issues. See Juliet B. Schor, *The Overworked American: The Unexpected Decline of Leisure* (New York: Basic Books, 1991).

53. See Joseph L. Badaracco, Jr., and Richard R. Ellsworth, *Leadership and the Quest for Integrity* (Boston: Harvard Business School Press, 1989), pp. 201–202.

54. See Laurent A. Daloz, *Effective Teaching and Mentoring: Realizing the Transformative Power of Adult Learning Experiences* (San Francisco: Jossey-Bass, 1986).

55. See G. Roche, "Much Ado About Mentors," *Harvard Business Review* (January–February 1979), pp. 14–28; and E. Shapiro, F. Haseltine, and M. Rowe, "Moving Up: Role Models, Mentors, and the 'Patron System,'" *Sloan Management Review* 19 (1978), pp. 51–58.

56. Laurent A. Daloz, Cheryl H. Keen, James P. Keen, and Sharon

Daloz Parks, "Lives of Commitment: A Study," unpublished research in progress.

57. See Rosabeth Moss Kanter, *The Change Masters: Innovation and Entrepreneurship in the American Corporation* (New York: Simon & Schuster, 1983), esp. pp. 304–305.

58. See Sharon Daloz Parks, "Social Vision and Moral Courage: Mentoring a New Generation of Educators," *Cross Currents* 40, 3 (Fall 1990), pp. 350–367.

59. Perry London, "The Rescuers: Motivational Hypotheses About Christians Who Saved Jews from the Nazis," in J. Macaulay and L. Berkowitz, eds., *Altruism and Helping Behavior: Social Psychological Studies of Some Antecedents and Consequences* (New York: Academic Press, 1970).

60. The study at Darden has been particularly attentive to these dynamics. See Rosalyn Berne, "Managing Diversity: A Critical View," unpublished paper, Darden School of Business Administration, University of Virginia, 1992.

61. A few of the students remarked in their first interview that they were doubtful about the number of investment bankers the world needs. This may, however, reflect not only ethical sensitivity but also the decline of opportunities in investment banking.

62. Tom Wolfe, "Cry of the '90s: 'Yes, It's Good, But for What?'" *Boston Globe,* February 18, 1990, pp. A25–27.

63. See Allan Bloom, *The Closing of the American Mind* (New York: Simon & Schuster, 1987).

64. See London, "The Rescuers"; and Douglas K. Huneke, *The Moses of Rovno* (New York: Dodd, Mead, 1985), p. 182.

65. Cf. p. 35.

66. See Kenneth Keniston, *Youth and Dissent: The Rise of a New Opposition* (New York: Harcourt Brace Jovanovich, 1960), p. 7.

67. See C. Roland Christensen, David A. Garvin, and Ann Sweet, eds. *Education for Judgment: The Artistry of Discussion Leadership* (Boston: Harvard Business School Press, 1991).

68. See Caroline Whitbeck, "The Trouble with Dilemmas: Rethinking Applied Ethics," *Professional Ethics* 1, 1 & 2, (Spring–Summer, 1992).

CHAPTER THREE

Engaging the Power and Competence of the Faculty

MARY C. GENTILE

From the earliest planning stages of the Leadership, Ethics, and Corporate Responsibility (LECR) initiatives at the Harvard Business School, those involved were very aware of both the benefits and the risks of its fortunate timing. As described in Chapter One, historical, social, demographic, and media trends had conspired to create a societal interest in, and even a demand for, greater attention to issues of business ethics and values in management education programs. Institutional realities at Harvard, such as the presence of strong and committed leadership, a dedication to instructional development, and alumni support, created a window of opportunity for this effort. On the other hand, unless effective measures were taken to institutionalize this effort and to weave its design deep into the fabric of the school's program, it could easily lose momentum as other equally pressing agendas came into the foreground—for the school, and for graduate business education more generally.

In order for this initiative to have the hoped-for broad and long-term impact on the school and its curriculum, ethical analysis and values-based decision making had to be the subject of new empirical research, decision-model building, and case study and course development across the whole curriculum. These had to become an integral part of the way the task of management was defined and taught. A broad-based and integrative effort to construct a cohesive educational and social

73

experience that placed questions of responsible and ethical behavior at the center of the MBA experience would have to be
designed (see Chapter Four). Thus every aspect of this effort
would be dependent ultimately on the support and energy of
the school's faculty.

With faculty commitment critical to the LECR initiative, it
was necessary to understand the responses, both positive and
negative, of individual faculty and to use this information to
guide program design and implementation. Consequently,
faculty concerns and interests relative to the role of values in
management education were explored through an extensive
series of conversations with senior and junior faculty from all
disciplines and within all areas of the school. Where the faculty
were resistant, understanding their resistance offered a correc-
tive to earlier, less successful efforts to integrate explicit discussions of values into the curriculum. Where the faculty were
supportive or even impatient, their support and eagerness
were a resource to be tapped.

Soliciting Senior Faculty Leadership

Central to the faculty outreach was Professor Thomas R. Piper, senior associate dean for Educational Programs, whose
visible leadership delivered an important message of school
commitment and whose senior management position in educational operations prevented faculty from perceiving the effort as marginal. As early as 1987, Dean Piper was initiating
conversations with faculty leaders, individually and in groups.
Some individuals were approached because of an expressed interest in or commitment to values-related issues; Professor
John Matthews, for example, had offered a business ethics
module in executive education programs for many years. Others were approached because they held positions of leadership
in major school programs—the faculty director of the MBA
Program, for example—or because of their visibility as respected teachers and outstanding scholars in the various func-

tional areas. Those perceived to be the "toughest sells" on the LECR initiative were also approached because their involvement would send a powerful signal to the rest of the school community, as well as provide invaluable insights into the potential pitfalls of the endeavor. A concerted effort was made to include faculty from as many functional areas as possible: Finance, Marketing, General Management, Production and Operations Management, Human Resource Management, and so forth.

Concurrently with this faculty outreach, Dean Piper met with the board of directors of the Associates of the Harvard Business School and the Visiting Committee, two influential groups of alumni and friends of the school that regularly share feedback and guidance. The viewpoints and enthusiastic support of these bodies were reported to the entire faculty in a formal presentation in May 1987, in which Dean Piper presented an outline of the initial planning for the LECR initiative and sought input and support from the faculty.

Faculty conversations during this period covered a variety of topics: Who were the school's students? What, if anything, did they need with regard to training in ethical management and responsible leadership? How had the field of business ethics been defined in the past? Was this definition consistent with the faculty's sense of what was needed in the MBA curriculum? How had these issues been approached by management schools in the past? Had they succeeded, and why or why not? These discussions—fueled by the results of a literature review and nationwide field research that produced reports on current and historical efforts of leading graduate business schools to integrate ethics into their curricula, and on the state of the discipline of business ethics as perceived by leading academics and scholars in the field—triggered such additional research as the study of students reported on in Chapter Two.

Eventually, a core group of senior faculty was assembled into an ad hoc committee. As will be seen repeatedly in the telling of this story, the effort to tap faculty insight served to generate faculty commitment as well. In fact, not only was the concept of and commitment to a required module on "Decision Making and Ethical Values" first articulated by this committee, but also the first teaching group for the actual module grew out of this early group (see Chapter Four).

Positive results notwithstanding, the early committee meetings were sometimes highly charged; some faculty who were openly skeptical believed the best service they could offer was their strongly expressed reservations. The presence of their voices, however discouraging at times, was critical to ensuring the initiative's relevance and realism.

Outreach to Faculty in the First-Year Required Curriculum: The Genesis of the "Barriers Report"

Concurrently with wide-ranging conversations about the LECR effort among senior faculty, an effort was made to understand the responses and concerns of the wider teaching faculty. Initially, attention was focused on those teaching in the first-year required curriculum, as these courses were the foundation of the MBA program and the training ground for entering faculty. Among these courses were Business, Government, and the International Economy; Competition and Strategy; Financial Reporting and Managerial Accounting; Finance; Human Resource Management; Managerial Economics; Management Communication; Information, Organization, and Control; Marketing; Organizational Behavior; and Technology and Operations Management.

Each incoming class of approximately 800 students is divided into nine sections of about ninety students each, who proceed through the required first-year curriculum together. The professors who teach all the sections of a particular course—Marketing, for example—constitute a "teaching group." Teaching groups, each led by a senior faculty member or "course head," meet regularly to plan the syllabus and develop teaching plans for each class.

Early in 1987, an audit was made of all first-year, required courses in the MBA curriculum to identify what ethical, or explicitly values-based, issues were already addressed in the course material, as well as to pinpoint additional ethical issues appropriate for incorporation into these courses. A research associate surveyed all the teaching groups for these courses, by telephone or face-to-face, thereby providing a nonthreatening introduction to subsequent conversations about the LECR initiative and generating a useful list of ethics-related business case studies. The audit recognized the teaching faculty's "ownership" and expertise regarding its own courses, thereby encouraging faculty to think creatively about the intersection of ethical issues and their curriculum objectives. Faculty were often surprised by the number of opportunities for ethical discussion already present in their courses.

Although this survey turned up the obvious issues of misconduct associated with the words "business ethics"—bribes, distorted financial statements, insider trading, deceptive advertising—faculty rather quickly moved beyond questions of misconduct or "thou shalt not" to questions of obligation or "thou shalt," and to organize these issues into challenges to the individual, the organization, the industry, or the political and economic system. New case study topics were generated. The process of reflection on curriculum development had begun.

The first-year required course audit not only provided a useful preliminary map of the ethical issues most appropriately addressed in each of the functional areas of the management curriculum, but also raised some underlying questions and concerns, uneasiness, hopes, and expectations associated with the LECR effort. Clearly there was much to learn from the responses of faculty, so one year later, during the first quarter of 1988, Dean Piper commissioned a series of in-depth (1–1½-hour) interviews with a significant number (about thirty individuals or approximately thirty-five percent) of the faculty who taught courses in the required first-year curriculum of the MBA program. These are the courses to which all students are exposed; they are the building blocks of the students' management education and establish in their minds the school's values and expectations. A representative sample of junior and senior faculty with a wide range of backgrounds was subsequently selected to be interviewed by Dr. Mary C. Gentile, a member of the LECR team who was familiar with the curriculum and known and trusted by many of the faculty. Over the next four years, Gentile would work to integrate ethics into the MBA program through new case and teaching plan development, faculty workshop and seminar design, and individual and group presentations; this study of faculty attitudes and insights laid the foundation for this ongoing work.

Although the working title of the study Piper commissioned was the "Barriers Report" (it was supposed to identify barriers to gaining faculty support for the LECR initiative), it quickly became apparent that the interviews were revealing levers as well as barriers, opportunities as well as obstacles. What looked like resistance to the LECR effort from one perspective became an expression of individual faculty integrity when viewed from another. However valuable these interviews were in guiding the design and implementation of the LECR initiative, the single most important lesson they provided was the guiding principle of respect for the experiences and insights of faculty.

The Barriers Report addressed two key questions:

1. What barriers to the integration of ethical discussion into the first-year MBA curriculum are experienced by faculty?
2. What are the implications of these barriers for the school's efforts to involve faculty in the LECR initiative?

The report included a brief profile of the distinctive culture and curriculum realities of each of the required management courses, as revealed by a comparison of consistencies and differences among faculty perceptions. For example, the relative lengths of courses, technical level of material covered, typical backgrounds of faculty in particular course areas, and course traditions concerning openness to experimentation could all affect the receptiveness of a particular teaching group to the LECR initiative. These profiles provided guidelines for customizing the design of later faculty workshops on business ethics and identified the strategies that would communicate most powerfully.

The interviews began with a number of questions about teaching in general, designed to elicit faculty conceptions of the model class discussion. Knowing these models, it was easier to understand faculty members' concerns about the way discussions of business ethics might affect their ideals. The interview also included questions designed to elicit from the faculty what "business ethics" meant to them. Finally, specific questions were asked about the role business ethics might or should play in faculty members' courses.

It was particularly appropriate to open these conversations with discussions of teaching, as the school's culture strongly emphasizes the importance of attention to pedagogy. Faculty are already mindful of this area, which receives considerable attention through established faculty development programs, such as the twelve-week faculty seminar "Teaching by the Case Method," offered each year to new teachers. Helping faculty to see the bridge between the LECR initiative and the development of a constructive learning environment in the classroom helped align this initiative with established priorities at the school.

The Barriers Report

This interview and research process led to the Barriers Report, which described fourteen barriers to, or necessary conditions for, wide participation of the faculty in the integration of ethical discussion into the required MBA curriculum. But each barrier in turn suggested levers or opportunities for action.

Barrier 1. *Assumptions about the definition of business ethics*

Many of the faculty interviewed defined business ethics solely or primarily in terms of an *individual's* choices or decisions and their impact upon other individuals. This definition had several implications:

    a. It suggested that many of the topics discussed in the MBA curriculum were irrelevant to, or beyond the scope of, ethical discussion because they were centered around the role, purpose, and behavior of an organization rather than an individual.

    b. It triggered faculty concerns that ethical discussion would in all cases involve discussion of personal belief and value systems. Theoretically and historically based discussions of public policy and ideology assumptions were not usually considered part of the business ethics terrain.

    c. It could generate irreconcilable tensions between the lessons of a particular course and the lessons of business ethics so defined, since the lessons of a course were often directed toward the choices, survival, and prosperity of a firm rather than an individual.

Some faculty saw discussions of business ethics as pitting the integrity and well-being of the individual against the integrity and well-being of the organization, rather than attempting to balance and reconcile the two. Faculty who defined business ethics primarily in terms of attention to managerial misconduct perceived the field to offer only restrictions to managerial choice, in a context in which confident, decisive action was prized. Other faculty viewed business ethics as a doctrine of altruism that had little to do with the competitive realities of the marketplace, or saw the introduction of business ethics into the management curriculum as little more than an invitation to sermonize in the classroom.

Lever. A broad definition of business ethics was needed, with a model of the discipline's terrain that included all areas of decision making: individual, organizational, and systemic

Figure 3.1

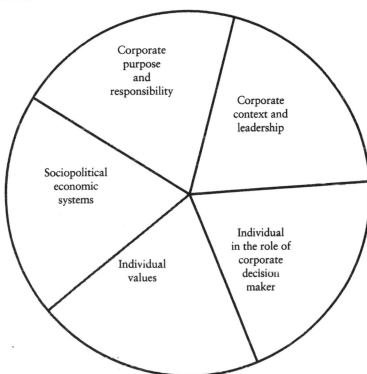

(see Figure 3.1). It was also necessary to focus on the proactive possibilities of ethical decision making by presenting examples of outstanding organizational practice, as well as more typical cautionary tales. Discussion of business ethics needed to be tied clearly to day-to-day business decisions and action planning, rather than perceived as a matter only of philanthropic gestures and sermonettes. Field research, as well as written and video case studies, were a natural format for these purposes.

Barrier 2. *Assumptions about the school's goals with regard to business ethics*

Many faculty seemed confused about the expected goals or

outcomes of integrating ethics into the MBA classroom. Many believed that the goal was to "change student behavior." This view triggered the refrain that graduate business students are already adults and a school cannot expect and should not try to change their value systems. It also engendered discomfort at the prospect of being expected to indoctrinate students with a particular viewpoint or ethical perspective. Most faculty seemed more comfortable with the notion of encouraging students to be aware of the ethical implications of their business decisions, to recognize the significance of these implications, and to apply particular modes of reasoning to these decisions, as opposed to telling students what the "good" or "right" decision would be. Some faculty feared that they would be asked to teach ethics as a distinct subject, and this triggered considerable and understandable resistance in some, who contended that they were not philosophers, that they should not be expected to learn a new discipline, that they were not equipped for such a task, and so forth.

Lever. It was necessary to arrange opportunities for the teaching faculty to discuss Parks's research findings on student value formation, illustrating that student priorities and value commitments are still very much in process, and underscoring their readiness and need for faculty mentoring (see Chapter Two). Additionally, it was necessary to provide faculty with classroom examples of what it looked like to integrate ethical considerations into the teaching of managerial decision making. They needed the opportunity to observe accomplished faculty from the full range of curricular areas teaching managerial case studies which introduced questions of ethical decision making. It was necessary to develop and distribute models of case studies and teaching plans which integrated ethical issues into the financial or marketing aspects of the business-planning process. Little would be accomplished if ethics was perceived as separate from the practical realm of management. And finally, the school's goals regarding ethics needed to be communicated clearly, repeatedly, and with concrete illustrations (e.g., faculty seminars, classroom observation). It was essential to demonstrate the difference between teaching that ethical commitment is an important and necessary part of a manager's responsibility, as opposed to teaching a set of "answers" to a particular list of ethical dilemmas. The school was committed to the former task.

Barrier 3. The need for a visible system of faculty incentives that encouraged attention to ethical issues in each functional area

Faculty who perceived the academic reward system to be based primarily on short-term, quantifiable results—the number of case studies written or articles published, for example—were skeptical of pursuing a line of inquiry with which they were unfamiliar and that produced results for which there were fewer publishing outlets. And even if they were successful in producing published material, they were not confident such research would be valued by their peers in the review process. Fundamentally, faculty were asking the school to ask itself, "What are the opportunity costs to us of turning our attention and time to business ethics?" They needed to see models of how to succeed in this endeavor.

Lever. Hiring individuals who produced quality research in the field of business ethics would send a strong signal. Equally if not more important, it was necessary to provide incentives, such as research assistance, to faculty in traditional functional areas who were integrating values-related questions into their research. It was important to encourage opinion leaders in these functional areas to support, through the mentoring and promotion process, those faculty who wished to pursue such research. Needless to say, this was seen as an incremental process, to be pursued through repeated formal and informal conversations among senior faculty.

Barrier 4. The need for new research—field research and theory building at the intersection of ethics and each of the functional areas— as a foundation for substantive teaching

Faculty who lacked confidence that they understood how practicing managers viewed ethical questions or the positive and negative implications of ethical viewpoints were uncomfortable about raising such issues in the classroom. In addition, faculty yearned for decision rules and/or frameworks comparable to those applied in other functional areas (e.g., discounted cash flows, rate-of-return calculations, breakeven analysis). They believed that purely speculative conversations or sermons did a disservice to both students and subject matter.

Lever. This need for research could begin to be satisfied in a variety of ways: for example, through research assistance to faculty in the traditional functional areas who agreed to integrate ethical issues into classroom analysis, and through the hiring of faculty who would focus on cross-disciplinary research. The latter had to be guided by the principle that new faculty would pursue managerially focused, field-based research aimed at integrating the theory of business ethics with the management practice. In addition, it became important to identify those analytic tools appropriate to ethical analysis (e.g., stakeholder analysis, rights-based analysis, utilitarian analysis), as well as to stress the limitations of any decision rule or framework applied badly, inconsistently, or out of context. Finally, the point had to be made that in fact few functional areas have foolproof formulas. In fact, in the school's experience, *all* the management disciplines are about teaching judgment and critical thought—and ethics offers an invaluable opportunity to do just that.

Barrier 5. *The perception that classroom norms inhibited the climate of trust and cooperation necessary for values-related discussion*

No matter how individual faculty members described their teaching style—and there was a wide degree of variance—there seemed to be an assumption among them that the MBA classroom norm was a highly competitive, interrogational forum that appeared, at least to the students, to pit one against the other. Faculty observed that students learned to defend their positions no matter what arguments were advanced by other students. Such defensive posturing could inhibit learning for students who believed that they could not change their minds without losing face.

This assumed classroom norm could impede the development of trust between faculty and students as well as between students. Some faculty were uncomfortable with students who had a reputation for being intelligent, articulate, and highly aggressive, just as some students were uncomfortable with faculty who had a reputation for being aggressively confrontational. It was difficult to gauge how many faculty actually adopted such a teaching style. In describing their styles, most faculty expressed true awareness of and concern for students' feelings. It seemed, however, despite repeated evidence of positive relationships in individual class sections, that widespread belief in this classroom phenomenon was significant in itself. Faculty observed that, particularly in values-based discussions, trust was essential for individuals to want to discuss their personal positions. In its absence, both faculty and students were likely to avoid controversial subjects in which they lacked expertise.

Faculty also raised a number of teaching questions specifically related to the discussion of ethics in the management classroom. For example:

- How should a faculty member respond to a student comment that appears blatantly unethical?

- Should a faculty member take a stand on an ethical issue in the classroom?

- How can a faculty member lead a discussion of common but questionable business practices without seeming to condone them, without seeming naive, and without appearing to instruct students in how to perform them?

Lever. Faculty's concern about pedagogy in general, and in particular the teaching of business ethics, provided an opportunity to associate the LECR initiative with addressing a felt need for more assistance with teaching challenges. It was necessary to focus on both the pedagogical implications of integrating business ethics into the curriculum and the need for new research and case development. The in-depth interviews with faculty teaching in the required curriculum generated a valuable list of teaching challenges (see Figure 3.2). Workshops and written materials were needed to help prepare faculty for these challenges. In addition, attention had to be paid to the development of a trusting classroom climate, conducive to all types of learning.

Barrier 6. *An awareness that the integration of ethics into the curriculum would require faculty to re-examine their own value systems*
This prospect triggered resistance for a variety of reasons.

a. Some faculty resisted recognizing the role they might already be playing, implicitly or explicitly, in shaping student value systems. They preferred to view their role as value neutral.
b. Some faculty were uncomfortable because they did not know where they stood on a variety of tough business ethics dilemmas, and expected that they should be certain of their position before they tried to lead discussions of such issues.
c. Some faculty were ambivalent about whether their own value systems, in fact, fit within a business school context. They were unclear about what such a school's true perspective should be with regard to its own purpose and the purpose of the firm (e.g., maximization of shareholder wealth, or a broader view of responsibility to stakeholders).

Lever. It was necessary to provide a variety of contexts in which faculty might discuss these issues one on one and in

Figure 3.2
Frequently Described Pedagogical Challenges in Ethical
Decisions

- Ethical discussions are so unpredictable in their timing and focus that it is difficult to have adequate teaching plans.

- Ethical discussions always seem like a digression from the subject at hand. They may be important issues, but don't seem to belong in the functional courses.

- Students often seem to want answers and faculty don't have them.

- How can a faculty member move the students beyond mouthing platitudes? Many faculty noted that the school's recent attention to ethics leads some students to raise these issues merely because they think it is what the faculty want to hear.

- Can faculty use humor in a discussion of ethical concerns without trivializing the issue?

- How can faculty encourage students to look beyond their gut reaction to an ethical dilemma and to think analytically, as they do on other issues?

- Because faculty cannot rely on technical expertise in an ethical discussion, some feel they need greater logical reasoning and debating skills in order to guide these discussions effectively.

- Because faculty often do not have analytic models to apply, they often complain that ethical discussions lack direction, feel pointless, and risk being "flat."

- How can faculty push students beyond superficial or abstract ethical observations to a more practical level of discussion?

- How can faculty move beyond their own embarrassment over discussions of ethics and personal values?

continued

Faculty are subject to the same peer pressures, imagined and real, that students are, and ethics is an issue that brings out vulnerabilities. Some faculty are afraid that their students will not take them seriously if they raise these issues. (This perception is tied to the expectation that faculty will be tough and brutally realistic and to the assumption that ethical discussions are by nature soft and idealistic.)

- Students who raise ethics questions may be "typed" by other students as "class angels"; it is sometimes suspected that they raise these issues because they can't contribute to the "real" course content. This encourages a lack of integration between the traditional course content and ethics.

- Discussing ethics in the classroom is "like playing with a loaded gun." It raises questions about whether one is a "good person"; ironically, students may simply learn to say the "right words" as a result.

- How can students and faculty learn to tolerate and work through values-based conflicts in class discussions?

groups, with their peers and across functional areas. It was important, especially for junior faculty, that some of these conversational contexts be free of faculty responsible for reviewing their work.

Barrier 7. *A variety of factors—age, experience, and familiarity with the case method of teaching, combined with individual perceptions of faculty role and value in the classroom—could affect faculty's willingness to integrate ethics into their classes*

Although many faculty, both senior and junior, believed that age, experience in the classroom, knowledge of the course material, and exposure to the case method affected willingness to deal with ethics in the classroom, no consistent pattern emerged. For example, some senior faculty suggested that junior faculty were probably less comfortable altering a prepared teaching plan to pursue a timely but unanticipated discussion of ethical issues. On the other hand, several junior faculty members recounted experimentation with trying to integrate ethics into their classes. One new faculty member explained that he felt he had little to lose by making changes, since he expected to make a lot of mistakes in his first class anyway. Another suggested that senior faculty might be more tied to proven teaching plans and less willing to abandon something they were confident worked. (Most of these assumptions were premised on the expectation that discussions of ethics would be unplanned and unprepared.)

Although all of the foregoing factors (age, expertise, experience with the case method) were mentioned and appeared to play some role in the experiences of the faculty interviewed, the most critical factor affecting willingness to address ethics in the classroom seemed to be how faculty defined their role and value in the classroom. (Such definitions are, of course, subject to change with age and experience.) For example, faculty who defined their value and comfort in the classroom as deriving directly from expertise or superior knowledge tended to be more uncomfortable with ethics unless they believed they had an analytic model to apply to such discussions, or were confident that they had thought through the issues in question and knew where they stood and why. In contrast, faculty who defined their value and comfort in the classroom as deriving not only from their knowledge in the field but also more directly from their facility with group processes and discussion leading expressed less concern about the idea of ethical discussions, and more about the difficulties of open, honest communication among faculty and students in the classroom context, about both case content, and also about the immediate classroom dynamics. Such faculty seemed more willing to explore ethical questions with their students in real time, as opposed to having a set perspective before discussion began.

Lever. Once again, awareness of these issues provided a mandate to focus on both research and pedagogy in faculty development efforts. Faculty who reflected the first of the two perspectives presented above tended to be interested in new research—field research and theory building—in the area of management ethics, whereas faculty who reflected the second placed greater emphasis on the challenge of managing class-room dynamics in discussions of business ethics.

Barrier 8. *The need for course heads and teaching groups to establish a receptive and encouraging context for developing teaching plans that integrated ethical issues into course content*

Since new faculty regularly taught in the first-year curricu-lum during their first two to four years at the school alongside more experienced teachers, teaching groups were important mentoring communities for almost a third of the faculty. Moreover, commitment of the course head to the integration of ethical issues into the curriculum was critical for signaling the real significance of these issues at the school.

Lever. As mentoring contexts, teaching groups provide powerful opportunities for raising awareness and creating norms among new and continuing faculty around the integra-tion of ethics into the management curriculum. Therefore the selection of course heads committed to values-related discus-sions represented another opportunity to send strong signals concerning the school's commitment to the LECR initiative.

Barrier 9. *Efforts to increase attention to ethics in the curriculum could be perceived by faculty as a form of reproach*

Some faculty (and students) expressed resentment and re-sistance to the idea that they needed to pay more attention to ethics. Once again, this response was often tied to the belief that business ethics was primarily about potential or perceived misconduct rather than about a wider conception of the roles, rights, and responsibilities of business organizations and busi-ness managers.

Lever. This reaction suggested the necessity of positioning the LECR effort in a broader educational and societal context (see Lever associated with Barrier 1); of emphasizing the importance of new research and theory building as opposed to proselytizing; and of listening to and acknowledging the validity and integrity of faculty and student reactions to the effort. If the LECR initiative was to be effective, particularly among faculty, it was critical that it not be positioned as a remedial effort, but instead engage the faculty's intellectual curiosity and commitment to teaching.

Barrier 10. *Faculty's mixed feelings about their status as personal role models*

Many faculty who identified strongly with their role as experts and enjoyed their status as role models with regard to their subject matter did not feel the same sense of mastery over values-related issues. Integration of ethics into the classroom could threaten the self-confidence of such faculty. Other faculty who resisted the concept of being a role model of any sort for students found that the integration of ethics into the classroom made it more difficult to deny this status. Faculty who were most at ease in more comradely relationships with their students were fearful that the discussion of ethics might place them in an uncomfortable role. This was especially true to the degree that faculty perceived the raising of ethics issues as an exclusively normative exercise—a sort of reproach—rather than an extension of the case analysis.

Lever. Through discussion of the teaching process and of Parks's research findings, faculty could become more aware of the influence they wielded with students, intended or not.

Barrier 11. *The perception that a tightly packed curriculum left little room for adding ethical material*

This barrier, although based on valid observations of an already crowded curriculum, seemed something of a red herring. Faculty would raise this objection initially, but then go on to explain their discomfort with ethical subject matter or their difficulty generating rigorous ethical discussion in the classroom. This objection also appeared to be tied to a faculty perception of student demand for practical tools and functional learning.

Lever. The question of time would be mitigated if ethics discussions could be raised to the intellectual level of the rest of the course, or could be adequately integrated into other discussions so they seemed less of a digression.

Barrier 12. *The compartmentalization of knowledge in the curriculum served as a barrier to the integration of ethics*

Because ethical implications of a particular business decision often extend beyond the more narrowly defined limits of a specific functional analysis, faculty in one area often suggested that an ethical issue might be more appropriately addressed in another course. Thus ethics issues could fall between the courses.

Lever. To effectively address major ethical concerns in management seemed to require some cross-functional coordination. Accordingly, it was desirable to exploit synergies between the LECR initiative and existing groups and committees that worked to promote a more integrated curriculum (e.g., the Required Course Subcommittee, a group that comprises the course heads for all required courses, and the Interfunctional Lunch Group, an informal gathering of faculty who meet regularly to share interfunctional research projects and generate ideas for promoting greater cross-fertilization of ideas).

Barrier 13. *Many faculty were not clear about what could and should happen in an effective discussion of business ethics, they were unclear about what their classroom goals should be and how to measure success*

Many faculty saw ethics as a "soft," idealistic, abstract, and even nebulous subject. They had never seen tools of moral reasoning applied to business situations and had no models. Because they did not know how to tie ethical issues into a business analysis, they sometimes tried to "save these discussions for last." Consequently, ethical considerations frequently fell victim to time constraints or were construed as something to be discussed after the fact. In the latter case, students were likely to have already formed their opinions of the problem at hand and thus were no longer feeling the same energy around the ethical issue they might have experienced earlier in the discussion.

Faculty also noted that they were not certain what standards they should set when leading and evaluating a values-related discussion. Should they aim for rigor? For empathic understanding? For both? How should they evaluate student contributions?

Lever. It was essential that faculty be afforded opportunities to audit class discussions in the required course module (see Chapter Four), and that business-ethics-related materials be included in the various faculty training programs (e.g., the Teaching by the Case Method seminar or the General Management Program, a one-week orientation to the school and the MBA curriculum held each August for all new faculty). In addition, discussion among faculty most experienced in leading business ethics classes (members of the teaching group for the required module, for example) could provide a forum for developing standards for evaluating such conversations.

Barrier 14. Discussion of the ethical issues in a case study seemed dangerous to some faculty because it could lead to discussion and questioning of the classroom process itself

Encouraging students to question ethical issues could empower them to raise questions about course material choices or classroom dynamics. Many faculty commented that this looking beyond the case was a good thing, but they also noted that it made them nervous.

Lever. Once again, the LECR initiative provided a focus and incentive for the school to address the teaching process itself and exploit potentially valuable synergies with existing faculty training programs.

Turning the Levers into Principles to Guide Faculty Involvement

Faculty input, together with the potential levers or strategies for change suggested by that input, were summarized in a number of principles that guided the school's efforts to draw faculty into the LECR initiative.

Definition

First, it was important to define the effort more broadly than "business ethics." "Leadership, Ethics, and Corporate Responsibility" was adopted as the title of the effort, in the conscious hope that it would suggest a focus that extended beyond attention to individual behavior to the examination of organizational responsibility for policy and culture building and the influence of legal, regulatory, political, economic, and social systems on managerial ethics. Rather than emphasizing potential misconduct exclusively, the effort also would focus attention on proactive management practice and the use of ethical analysis to reveal opportunities for positive action. Finally, the role of ethical analysis in the actual process of decision making was to be emphasized by encouraging field research and case study development.

Integration

Second, it was clear that without a concerted effort to integrate discussion of values-related issues across the curriculum, the power of the prevailing models of analysis and assumptions regarding the relevant facts and constituencies in any managerial decision would drown out any stand-alone effort to address the wider questions of leadership, ethics, and corporate responsibility. Unless faculty were drawn into the process of addressing these issues, their doubts about the definition and importance of business ethics as part of the curriculum would be sufficient to trigger students' skepticism regarding its relevancy.

Specialization

Third, it became apparent that introducing faculty to a set of generic issues and models for ethical analysis in business would be insufficient. Instead, intellectual specialization would be necessary. Innovative and rigorous research, going far beyond broad mandates for responsible management and focusing on the specific and specialized interests of different functional areas, would be necessary to engage faculty intellectually and build a solid foundation for curriculum additions. Analysis of faculty interview data yielded a list of values-related issues appropriate to each functional course area. For example, professors in Business, Government and the International Economy, suggested that questions of ethnocentric and conflicting definitions of fair competition were relevant. Faculty in Competition and Strategy raised questions about the ethical gathering and use of competitive information. (See Figure 3.3 for an extensive list.) In addition, faculty were encouraged to identify for each functional area conceptual paradigms and/or cultural norms that might constitute barriers to (or serve to encourage) the integration of ethics. For example, emphasis on technical or quantitative analytics in finance or control sometimes bred a classroom context less hospitable to more qualitative or subjective forms of analysis. In such instances, it was essential to develop case situations that relied on both quantitative and qualitative analysis to develop the most ethical, efficient, and effective plan of action. This specialized approach to research and course development ensured that the required MBA curriculum, when viewed as a whole, would address each aspect of the proposed map of the Leadership, Ethics, and Corporate Responsibility initiative. It also reassured faculty that they were being asked not to venture from their own fields of research and teaching, but rather to enhance them.

Figure 3.3
Examples of Ethical Issues in Particular Courses as Identified in Faculty Interviews

[This is by no means an exhaustive list of ethical issues, but rather a sampler of frequently mentioned examples.]

- BUSINESS, GOVERNMENT AND THE INTERNATIONAL ECONOMY
  - The question of equitable distribution of wealth and opportunity within a specific country
  - The question of political repression or freedom within a specific country
  - Issues of corruption and public trust in public policy
  - Questions of jurisprudence (e.g., when a firm based in one country operates in another, to whom is it accountable and for what?)
  - Differences in how individual countries define fair and unfair competition
  - Ethnocentricism

- COMPETITION AND STRATEGY
  - The gathering and uses of competitive information
  - The prioritization of criteria used in evaluating competitive strategy: for example, how heavily does one emphasize "value to the stakeholders" as compared to criteria focused exclusively on profit maximization?
  - The treatment of less-developed countries by firms with international competitive strategies (e.g., exploitation, stereotyping)
  - Collusion in markets
  - Plant closings and the firm's responsibility to the community
  - The definition of "fair" versus "unfair" competition

- CONTROL
  - Organizations systematically misstating information in their financial reporting and records
  - Fraud

- The importance of control systems in influencing employee behavior, for good or ill

● FINANCE

  - The topic of inside information, as relevant to both the firm's and individual manager's portfolios
  - Financial reporting: when one must report, how much one must report, and to whom
  - Securities fraud
  - The question of for whom the firm is run (i.e., the fiduciary responsibility versus a broader vision of responsibility to all stakeholders)

● HUMAN RESOURCE MANAGEMENT

  - The questions of layoffs and firings
  - Issues related to unions (e.g., responsibilities to employees, labor relations, labor negotiations)
  - Discrimination
  - Issues of employee privacy and confidentality: testing (drug, AIDS, psychological); grievances; impact of new technology on privacy; whistleblowing
  - Discussion of workers' and managers' rights
  - Executive compensation

● MANAGEMENT COMMUNICATIONS

  - Honesty in corporate communications
  - Manipulation of information and the media
  - Disclosure: how much? when? to whom?

● MANAGEMENT INFORMATION SYSTEMS

  - Descaling: the elimination of work functions through technology
  - Downsizing: the elimination of employee positions through technology
  - The impact of expert systems on individual responsibility and opportunity
  - Who will have access to technology?
  - Questions of anticompetitive behavior through technology (unnatural monopolies)

continued

- Questions around information: privacy, accuracy, property, access
- Ethics and public policy in information technology

- MARKETING
  - Decisions to market products of questionable safety or value to the consumer (cigarettes, "me-too" products, and so forth)
  - Dual loyalties when competitors cooperate in the market: Is one working for the firm, or for the industry as a whole?
  - Product design (safety, reliability, planned obsolescence)
  - Pricing: questions of fairness
  - Communications policy: honesty in internal and external communications (e.g., deceptive advertising)
  - Responsibilities to distributors
  - Coercive or deceptive sales tactics

- ORGANIZATIONAL BEHAVIOR
  - Manipulating versus motivating
  - Communicating and enforcing ethical standards within an organization
  - Resolving conflicts between the individual employee's value system and that of the organization
  - Managing diversity: creating an equitable, empowering corporate culture for all employees

- PRODUCTION AND OPERATIONS MANAGEMENT
  - Layoffs and firing as a strictly functional, standard operating procedure in managing production levels and expenses
  - The impact of technology on employees
  - Process safety
  - Responsibility for quality
  - Decision criteria for plant investment choices: short-term versus long-term thinking and the im-

plications for employees, consumers, and the environment
- Managing cultural, gender, and other differences among the work force

Pedagogy

Fourth, emphasis on the pedagogical challenges of integrating business ethics into the MBA curriculum would not only break down faculty barriers, but also identify the LECR initiative with an effort to address a perceived need on the part of faculty to enhance teaching skills. Faculty workshops and training materials needed to be developed and synergies with existing faculty training efforts nurtured.

Customization

Fifth, just as the LECR research agenda would need to be specialized to address the salient questions and take advantage of the analytic methods associated with each functional area, so efforts to involve faculty from each of the functional areas would need to be customized to suit the culture of each required course. Some groups were open to the idea of modifying their course structure and class sequence; others wanted to work within the constraints of the existing syllabus. The LECR initiatives had to be flexible, designed to build on faculty enthusiasm wherever and in whatever form it existed.

For example, some faculty were attracted to a particular ethical issue and appreciated resources and support in developing new materials to expand their existing syllabus into an entirely new area. In this way, the Management Information Systems faculty developed materials on the impact of information technology on privacy rights, while the Technology and Operations Management faculty developed cases on plant safety.

On the other hand, the Marketing faculty took a more structural approach to their syllabus, deciding to integrate some ethical material into each of the existing eight modules within their course syllabus. Rather than adopting an issue-driven approach to the task, they chose to actively seek out ethical questions which were embedded, but not currently addressed, in each aspect of the marketing mix.

Institutionalization

Finally, the LECR initiative had to be solidly institutionalized. Strong signals of commitment from the school's leadership, including career and resource incentives, would be needed to enable faculty to invest intellectually, professionally, and emotionally in the initiatives.

Staffing Objectives for Faculty Involvement

The success and continued growth of the LECR initiative were clearly in the hands of the school's faculty. An effective faculty development effort for this program would require a staffing plan as well as a set of interdependent signals, models, incentives, training programs, and resource allocation systems guided by the principles summarized above. Faculty responses to these efforts would have to be continually monitored so that programs could be revised and redesigned as faculty attitudes and needs changed.

For example, one of the strongest emphases in the first two years of the LECR effort was on new case development that integrated ethical issues into traditional courses. Faculty had to move beyond their concern that these issues could not be raised in the classroom and abandon their skepticism about whether the school was really serious about the ethics initiative. More recently, substantial energy has been devoted to new course development and the innovative research that will drive and be driven by such courses. This is a consequence of faculty beginning to be ready to look more deeply into the interface between values and their traditional interests. Initial skepticism is fading as faculty recognize a need to go beyond individual case situations to industry comparisons and theory building.

Three levels of faculty participation were deemed necessary if the LECR initiative was to take root.

1. A core group of (five to seven) *LECR core faculty* who focus on the various aspects of the field (see Figure 3.1) would be responsible for continuity and major course development in the required course module, Managerial Decision Making and Ethical Values These core faculty would pursue independent research on topics central to the area; develop and teach second-year electives, such as Moral Dilemmas of Management; Information, Power and Responsibility; Profits, Markets and Values; and The Business World: Moral and Social Inquiry Through Fiction; conduct collaborative research with faculty in other management functional areas; serve as inhouse consultants to faculty in other functional areas who request assistance with the development of teaching plans around business ethics issues; and develop expertise in the pedagogy of business ethics. These faculty would bring to their research and teaching a variety of backgrounds, including management, philosophy, the humanities, and law. The group would be built through strategic faculty hires and through the development of internal faculty who participated in the earlier planning committee and teaching group for the required module.

A variety of professional development programs established for this core group served both as intellectual stimuli and bonding experiences. For example, several members of the group participated in the universitywide one-year fellows program offered by the Program for Ethics and the Professions (see Figure 3.4), which brought faculty from various professional schools (e.g., business, law, medicine, public policy) together to discuss issues of applied ethics. Additionally, the Harvard Business School collaborated with the Program for Ethics and the Professions on the organization of seminars that addressed such topics as truth-telling and adversarial ethics. A collaboration between the Business School and the Harvard

Figure 3.4
Harvard Program in Ethics and the Professions

The Harvard Program in Ethics and the Professions encourages teaching and research about ethical issues in public and professional life. It is intended to meet the growing need for teachers and scholars who address questions of moral choice in business, government, law, or medicine. By bringing together those with competence in philosophical thought and those with experience in professional education, the program promotes a perspective on ethics informed by both theory and practice. Through its support of fellowships and other activities, the program seeks to develop a community of teachers and scholars dedicated to the study of ethics in the professions.

School of Divinity resulted in a faculty lunch seminar begun in 1991–1992. Eventually, the LECR interest group, as it became known by its third year, organized a regular biweekly lunch meeting to discuss members' research, joint projects, and future plans. This group designed a schoolwide faculty seminar series, offered for the first time in academic year 1991–1992, to provide a forum in which faculty could present new research and research in process. The seminar series also serves as outreach to the wider faculty community (see Figure 3.5).

2. A group of faculty from the various functional areas would serve as *bridges* or links between the required curriculum and the LECR core faculty. These bridge faculty would teach on a rotating basis for two- or three-year stints in the required ethics module in the first-year curriculum. While the LECR core faculty would provide continuity in the course module, the rotating faculty would help maintain its relevance to the rest of the MBA curriculum. The bridge faculty would be positioned to share their experiences and learning with colleagues in their home area, encouraging further integration of values-related issues into the rest of the required curriculum. Initially, senior faculty were identified as the most appropriate

---

Figure 3.5
Decision Making and Ethical Values Faculty Seminar
1991–1992

- International Trade in Hazardous Pesticides: Whose Responsibility?—Lynn Sharp Paine

- Four Spheres of Executive Responsibility—Joseph Badaracco

- The Role of Business in South Africa's Political and Economic Transition: A Case Study in the Savings & Loan Industry—Bruce Scott

- Public Goods and Private Interests in the Northwestern Forest Timber Industry—Forest Reinhardt

- Beliefs and Boundaries—Bob Simons

- Risk, Trust, and Startups—Amar Bhide

- Fairness in Business Relationships: Conversations with Entrepreneurs and Venture Capitalists—Greg Dees

- The Challenge of Ethical Discussions in the MBA Classroom: Student Assumptions and Faculty Paradigms—Mary Gentile

---

individuals to teach in the required module because their involvement sent a stronger signal to students and faculty, and their teaching experience in the MBA classroom served the module well.

A second group of bridge faculty, the course heads for the required first-year courses, were asked by Dean Piper and through conversations with Gentile to lead the effort to integrate values-related issues into their courses through the development of new cases and teaching plans that address ethical issues embedded in existing course material. As noted earlier, these course heads are powerful mentors for new faculty.

3. Finally, it was expected that *all faculty* would eventually share a basic competence and comfort addressing ethical and

values-based issues explicitly throughout the required curriculum and elective courses. This competence and comfort would develop over time through a variety of means described in the following section.

The Faculty Development Cycle

Meeting the faculty involvement and staffing objectives described above requires a complex set of signals, incentives, and programs. In earlier conversations with individual faculty, responses to the LECR initiatives had not been homogeneous; different faculty required different forms of motivation and support. Nor were faculty responses to the effort static; as the school context changed, faculty attitudes changed. But the success of these efforts, and their intellectual and pedagogical integrity, were entirely dependent on a willingness to listen to, respond to, and ultimately follow the faculty. Consequently, the following cycle of faculty involvement was set in motion with the expectation that different faculty would join one or more programs at different times.

The Required Module: Managerial Decision Making and Ethical Values

The objectives and expected impact of the required module upon the MBA curriculum and students are described in Chapter Four. But this module was also a central part of the faculty involvement effort.

First, as a course home for the LECR core faculty, it provides the legitimacy that derives from being part of the first-year required curriculum. It also provides a motivating and training ground for the faculty who will eventually become bridges between the LECR area and other functional areas. For example, care was taken that the module teaching group (nine professors) include faculty from as many different areas as possible (Finance, Marketing, Organizational Behavior, and so forth). These faculty serve as informal liaisons to the required first-year teaching group in each area. Gentile and Parks also participated in this group, providing insight gathered from their work with the faculty and students.

Finally, the new module sent a powerful signal to all faculty that the school is indeed serious about the LECR initiative. What's more, it created a strong motivation for faculty teaching in the other first-year courses to understand the materials their students would study in the module and to anticipate possible impacts upon their own course materials and class discussions. It was hoped (and in fact explicitly suggested) that students who spent their first three weeks addressing values-related issues in this module would feel encouraged to raise these questions in other courses. For some faculty, this was a welcome challenge; for others, it caused considerable anxiety. But overall, the sense that this material could not be ignored created an opportunity to develop materials and programs that responded to this interest.

At the start, for example, faculty from required course teaching groups were invited to audit a section of the module and thereby test their preconceptions about values-based discussions in the MBA classroom. Given this opportunity to observe senior faculty (faculty selected in part for their expertise with the case method of teaching) in action, they began to develop models for what these conversations could and should be like, thereby addressing one of the barriers discussed earlier.

The module teaching group serves not only as a source of models, but also as a sort of laboratory for discussing and refining the central terrain of business ethics and developing teaching strategies. Although the module meets for only three weeks at the beginning of each academic year, the teaching group continues to meet periodically throughout the year, developing goals for new course materials and discarding unsatisfactory materials. Among more recent goals for course development were: inclusion of more international case materials; development of a new case that addresses issues of fairness in responding to a diverse work force; inclusion of more cases that focus on the challenge of implementation as opposed to diagnosis of managerial and ethical problems.

Teaching group discussion extends beyond course module content to the goals of successful business–ethics classroom discussion. Teaching group members concerned about striking a balance between intellectual challenge and personal engagement have evolved an implicit teaching theory based on tenets such as the following:

- Students must feel safe in the classroom, secure in the belief that it is acceptable and desirable to be candid within explicitly stated bounds of mutual respect. Students who perceive that a "party line" is expected of them are not likely to engage at the deep emotional level required to generate genuine commitment and concern.

- Teaching methods ought to allow and encourage students to change their minds during the course of discussion (a notion faculty tried to validate by occasionally asking students to register their opinions on an issue at the start of class with a straw vote and then later vote again, often revealing pronounced shifts in general opinion).

- The power and immediacy of the module are enhanced by the use of experiential teaching tactics (such as role plays) and efforts to draw parallels between the cases discussed and students' current experience (for example, a discussion of corporate codes of conduct was concluded by sharing the school's code of conduct, discussing its implications, and encouraging students to develop their own class code).

Learning such as this is shared with the wider faculty through written teaching plans and informal discussion. Members of the module teaching group are also keenly aware that they are the first faculty to have contact with incoming MBA students, who form their initial and strongest impressions of the classroom process in this course. These first classes also provide a context within which each section of ninety students begins to build a community and to forge its group identity, an identity that will last throughout the entire first year since students take all their required courses with the same cohort. Thus module faculty felt a special responsibility to explicitly discuss the roles of trust and cooperation in the classroom as a balance to the perceived norm of competition in the classroom.

Customized Workshops for the Teaching Groups in the First-Year Curriculum

In response to the interest and occasional anxiety sparked by the introduction of the ethics module in 1988, a series of customized workshops was developed for nine of the eleven required first-year courses: Business, Government and the International Economy; Control; Finance; Management Communications; Management Information Systems; Managerial Economics; Marketing; Production and Operations Management; and Organizational Behavior. Interestingly, the two members of the LECR core faculty (Gentile and Kenneth Goodpaster) who developed these workshops had originally targeted as a pilot venture only two of the eleven first-year courses, but when word went out that such workshops were being developed, other teaching groups began to request attention.

These workshops introduced faculty in the required functional courses to the purposes and content of the new module, suggested potential synergies between the module and their own courses, and introduced teaching group faculty to the same models of ethical reasoning that students encountered in the module. They provided an opportunity for teaching groups to discuss the major ethical issues that surfaced in their own courses, to begin to develop strategies for addressing these issues effectively, and to identify intersections between LECR and their subject areas where more research and course development might be fruitful. Finally, the pedagogical challenges of values-related discussions were addressed.

Not every workshop focused on all these objectives. Prior to each workshop, members of the target teaching group were interviewed by Gentile in an effort to identify the greatest perceived needs and the intervention strategies that might be most effective with the particular group. Workshops ranged in length from two hours to an entire day. Some groups pursued general discussions of the proper place of explicit, values-related material in their courses; others, already convinced that values must be addressed, discussed particular case studies and developed effective teaching plans for introducing ethical questions.

The Marketing group, for example, identified four existing cases that seemed to present ethical questions. One concerned potentially coercive sales strategies used by a vacation timeshare real estate operation; another addressed the adoption of traditional marketing tactics by a not-for-profit hospital, raising questions about whether such measures were consistent with the public service commitment of such an organization. Gentile worked with the Marketing faculty to write new teaching plans that integrated the ethical issues with the existing teaching objectives for these cases. Each member of the teaching group left the workshop with new materials that could be applied in the classroom.

Other teaching groups brainstormed about needed new case development or discussed teaching process issues. Each workshop was facilitated by the course head of the particular teaching group, together with Gentile and Goodpaster.

As noted previously, new materials were often developed for use in these workshops. Sometimes, relevant articles were assembled in packets and bibliographies compiled to be distributed to faculty. As preparation for the Management Information Systems (MIS) workshop, Gentile and John Sviokla, an MIS faculty member, coauthored "Information Technology in Organizations: Emerging Issues and Policy," an article that provided faculty and students with a model for identifying and reflecting on the ethical implications of information technology. In addition, all faculty received copies of the syllabus and readings for the required ethics module.

In an effort to address the pedagogy of business ethics, Gentile developed a series of brief case vignettes based on faculty-identified teaching challenges generated by earlier discussions of ethics in the management classroom. These teaching scenarios were called "What Ifs": for example, "What if . . . a student raises a difficult ethical question, but it is in the middle of another very important discussion? If it were any other topic, the faculty member would not hesitate to postpone the comment, but since it is ethics, he or she worries about the message such a deferral may send." Each vignette was followed by a series of written suggestions concerning possible ways to deal with the situations that were used as the basis for discussion in many of the teaching group workshops.

The key strategy in developing these workshops was to work with faculty to develop materials that would be consistent with their existing teaching style and objectives. When the Production and Operations Management group was interested in the ethical implications of participative plant management schemes, the workshop provided background and suggestions for teaching about the implicit contracts employers established with employees in structuring these schemes. When the Organizational Behavior group was most concerned about skills in leading and focusing values-based discussions, Gentile sat in on classes and then ran discussion workshops to analyze different teaching tactics and whether or not they worked.

Teaching group faculty forged relationships with LECR core faculty that persisted throughout the year as the latter were invited to sit in on classes and work with faculty on further refinements of new teaching plans. At the close of the fall 1988 semester, debriefing meetings were held to assess whether and how class discussion had changed and to strategize about future efforts to integrate values-related material into the course. The hope and expectation are that collaboration between faculty teaching in other first-year courses and the LECR core faculty will continue, creating opportunities for joint research and course development.

Research Assistance

The faculty interviews and teaching group workshops described here afforded course heads for the required first-year courses an opportunity to identify the field research and case development efforts that would make the greatest and most immediate contribution to their curricula. As a course development agenda emerged, Dean Piper enlisted the cooperation of the school's research directors in securing resources, and research associates were made available for one year, on a full- or part-time basis, to assist interested course heads in writing new case studies and teaching plans that integrated ethical issues into their syllabi.

Each project was defined and designed by individual course heads and their teaching groups. In the Human Resource Management course, for example, a part-time researcher assisted faculty in the development of new case materials for a module on managing diversity—in particular, a case on the development of workplace policy concerning AIDS. Similarly, new materials that addressed the impact of information technology upon individuals' rights to privacy were developed for the Management Information Systems course. Materials developed for the Organizational Behavior course focused on managing potential conflicts between individual and organizational value systems. In Marketing, the course head and a visiting professor embarked on an ambitious project to develop a series of new cases that would highlight ethical dilemmas specific to each aspect of the marketing mix—distribution, communication, product policy, and pricing—thereby integrating ethics and values throughout the course. The course head of the Production and Operations Management course confided to an LECR core faculty member that, although the course was supposed to familiarize students with the challenges and responsibilities of the plant manager, it was not until she asked him about the ethical issues relevant to his course that he realized no attention was devoted to issues of plant and process safety. Chagrined at this realization, he embarked on a year-long project with a research associate to develop a case and teaching plan that addressed process safety in the semiconductor industry.

These were among the early projects that grew out of the initial collaboration between the LECR core faculty, other required-course faculty, and research associates. More recently, cases have been developed about discrimination in company promotion decisions, about the relationships between environmental responsibility and manufacturing strategy, about management responsibility in South Africa, and about honest and responsible accounting for loan loss reserves in the banking industry, to name a few. The effort is seen as a continuing process, with the expectation that several new cases that integrate ethical discussions into existing required courses in the first-year curriculum will be developed each year.

Seminars and Colloquia

Other forums besides individual faculty conversations and teaching group workshops also served to raise issues of integrating ethical discussions into the broader curriculum. Dean Piper and other faculty involved in the LECR effort often took advantage of existing programs to reach faculty. Beginning in 1987, Piper annually updated faculty about LECR efforts at the spring faculty meeting, and LECR core faculty speak at interdisciplinary lunches for junior faculty and at area research discussion meetings. As mentioned previously, several case studies from the required module were inserted into the General Management Program, an annual, week-long, new-faculty orientation to the school and the case method, and teaching challenges of values-related issues were discussed in the faculty seminar, Teaching by the Case Method.

Among new seminars and colloquia that were initiated was a school-sponsored Workshop on Ethics and Management

Education, held in December 1988, that brought business ethicists and philosophers, graduate school of management faculty, and business-school deans together to discuss the challenges of integrating ethics into the MBA curriculum. In June 1989, all interested faculty at the school were invited to attend a one-and-one-half-day internal seminar on the same topic. This seminar included case study discussions, faculty presentations of new materials from several of the first-year courses, and, perhaps most important, discussions of student reactions to these materials.

It was at the latter seminar that faculty received their first formal exposure to Parks's preliminary findings (reported in Chapter Two). By linking efforts to involve faculty in the LECR initiative with opportunities to learn more about who their students are, the seminar planners were able to respond to one of the faculty's central concerns: the need for more attention to teaching process and classroom dynamics.

Research colloquia have also been encouraged, including a conference on organizational deviance in spring 1989 (sponsored by Professor Rosabeth Kanter and Visiting Professor Amitai Etzioni) and the first annual international conference of the Society for the Advancement of Socioeconomics hosted at the school one month later. A research colloquium on marketing ethics (developed by Professors Ray Corey and John Quelch and Visiting Assistant Professor Craig Smith) was held in May 1990.

Such efforts are designed to stimulate interest among faculty whose interest might not have been stimulated by other efforts linked more closely to the first-year curriculum. It was hoped that as faculty attended programs such as these, some might become interested in teaching the required module, producing collaborative research with LECR core faculty, or helping to integrate ethics into second-year elective courses. Any and all of these activities would further expand the network of faculty involved in the initiative.

Remaining Challenges

After several years of work in the multiple initiatives described here, signs of progress were readily apparent. This obvious progress in turn helped involve more faculty in the LECR initiative. New case studies and teaching plans have been written; articles and books have been published, and others are under way; new second-year elective courses have appeared, and others are being developed (see Figure 3.6). The importance of visible products as a motivator of faculty involvement cannot be overstated.

Efforts to ensure a broad base of faculty commitment to the initiatives are necessarily still at an early stage. Although new materials have been added to almost all first-year courses, the

---

Figure 3.6
Visible Products: A Sampler

- **CASE DEVELOPMENT**
  A bibliography of business ethics teaching materials published in 1992 listed 136 case studies, 15 background notes, and 34 *Harvard Business Review* reprints. More than two-thirds of those cases and notes were developed in the preceding three years.

- **COURSE DEVELOPMENT**
  For example:
  - *Decision Making and Ethical Values*: a three-week required module for new MBA students.
  - *Moral Dilemmas of Management*: a new second-year elective designed by Lecturer Joseph Badaracco.
  - *Information, Power and Responsibility*: a new second-year elective designed by Associate Professor Lynn Paine.
  - *Profits, Markets and Values*: a new second-year elective designed by Associate Professor J. Gregory Dees.

continued

- **PUBLICATIONS**
  For example:

  - *Managerial Decisions and Ethical Values*: course readings for the required module (edited by Kenneth E. Goodpaster and Thomas R. Piper), accompanied by an extensive Instructor's Manual (edited by Mary C. Gentile, Kenneth E. Goodpaster, and Thomas R. Piper).
  - *Ethics in Practice: Managing the Moral Corporation*, edited, with an introduction, by Kenneth R. Andrews.
  - *Leadership and the Quest for Integrity*, by Joseph L. Badaracco and Richard R. Ellsworth.

---

challenge of rethinking the basic assumptions and guiding paradigms of each functional area remains, and the much-needed new case development must eventually fail if it is not accompanied by field research and theory building. Finally, efforts to involve more faculty in the LECR initiative will falter if new research and more sophisticated teaching tactics are not continuously forthcoming.

New initiatives include the 1991–1992 LECR faculty seminar cited previously and ongoing interviews aimed at continually monitoring the concerns and needs of students. Discussions are under way to consider the development of a second required course module or required second-year course as a way to resurface the discussion of leadership, ethics, and corporate responsibility at a point near the end of the MBA program. Some faculty have suggested a new executive education program that addresses these topics. Changes in the doctoral program may also become necessary, if new faculty are to be trained in a blend of research and teaching that integrates managerial field-based research and scholarship with the tools and perspectives of business ethics.

So the process of faculty development must continue, guided by the principles derived from extensive and still ongoing conversations with the faculty themselves. A continuous feedback loop runs between the LECR core faculty who design these efforts and the rest of the school's management faculty. As interests, comfort levels, and intellectual trends change, so too must the faculty development program evolve. The efforts described in this chapter are presented in the hope that they may prove stimulating and useful to those faculty and administrators at other schools that are contemplating similar initiatives. Obviously, the choices made at the Harvard Business School were designed to respond to the particular needs and concerns of this school's faculty. Another school may choose very different strategies for involving its faculty in such a program. But if only one lesson were to be drawn from both the accomplishments and the remaining challenges at the school, it might be that the faculty themselves know best what is required for Leadership, Ethics, and Corporate Responsibility to become an integral part of the school's intellectual agenda.

CHAPTER FOUR

A Program to Integrate Leadership, Ethics, and Corporate Responsibility into Management Education

THOMAS R. PIPER

The business manager, particularly in the larger firm, possesses great power for good or harm, and public opinion demands that this power be exercised with responsibility, even though the goals to be served are not clearly discerned or generally agreed upon. . . In any event, the task calls for men [women] of broad knowledge and sensitive perception, with a well-developed philosophy and set of ethical values, and with the ungrudging willingness to accept the responsibilities inevitably associated with the possession of power.

Robert Gordon and James Howell, *Higher Education for Business* (New York: Columbia University Press, 1959), pp. 15–16.

Throughout the history of graduate management education, many faculties and deans have felt the desire and the obligation to convey a commitment to ethical business practice through their curriculum. This desire has been accompanied by constant debate and uncertainty as to how best to act on the conviction that ethical values, leadership, and corporate responsibility are matters of fundamental importance to the mission of a business school. Coupled with earlier failures and limited institutional commitments, this uncertainty led to initiatives and experiments that were tentative at best. An unsatisfactory cycle soon emerged. In a given era, efforts might be made to distribute these important issues across all courses. When that approach was assessed and found wanting, it would be abandoned and replaced by an elective course, marking a new phase in the cycle. When success again proved elusive, a required course might be attempted. And finally, going full circle, the broad-distribution approach might be revived.

This is not intended to disparage any such efforts. In most

cases, at schools across the country, these initiatives were undertaken by outstanding, courageous individuals. Unfortunately, the efforts were insufficient in relation to the totality of institutions and their cultures. By the mid-1980s, issues of ethics and corporate responsibility had been relegated to the periphery at most business schools. (A brief history of business ethics at the Harvard Business School is provided in Appendix I.)

In the late 1980s, a variety of external factors came together to create a fertile environment for redoubled efforts to address business ethics. As the United States struggled to remain competitive in the international economy, and as highly visible evidence of misconduct in business came to light, concern spread that mastery of management theory and analytic tools had eclipsed discussion of guiding purpose, principle, and responsibility in American business schools; that the pathfinding area—in which leadership, vision, imagination, and values converge—had been neglected.[1]

Many schools have responded. Harvard Business School, for example, has introduced a broad program of reinforcing initiatives in an effort to integrate these issues into the MBA experience.[2] These include a required course in the first year, discussion of ethical issues in the other courses that constitute the first year, a selection of electives in the second year, and efforts to surround the curriculum with opportunities to reflect upon and discuss issues and dilemmas with moral consequences.

The initiative is the product of long discussion, debate, and a studied consideration of antecedent efforts, both at Harvard and elsewhere (see Appendix II). It would be at least premature to assert that all of the necessary components are solidly in place and will endure, but the underlying beliefs and the program structure have been fairly tested. They are sufficiently sound to warrant sharing with colleagues so that productive conversations can continue.

Guiding Program Beliefs

Belief 1. *Ethics is as much an attitude as it is a set of skills and knowledge.*

No one can seriously challenge the importance of nurturing skills in listening, critical thinking, and moral reasoning; or of developing the analytics that enable managers to discern the nature and cause of ethical dilemmas and to assess the impact of decisions and decision-making processes on stakeholders; or of facilitating the understanding of conflicting views and of the constraints on managerial discretion and action. But one can question whether any such skills and knowledge will ever be called on in the absence of a set of related ethical attitudes and beliefs. If such attitudes and beliefs are indeed necessary, then one must assign to the following objectives a central place in management education:

- To depict business as a system of responsibilities, commitments, relationships, and purposes.

- To see relationships based on respect, honesty, fairness, and trust as fundamental to the effective and ethical functioning of organizations.

- To instill a recognition of a leader's responsibilities toward employees, customers, community, suppliers, and owners.

- To develop moral awareness in individuals who, while under severe time pressures, will be faced with a constant stream of decisions about situations that rarely come labeled as "ethical dilemmas."

- To inspire and empower students to imagine solutions— to envision a personal role in shaping a positive future.

- To challenge cynicism as a destructive unifying attitude and as a costly rationalization for inaction.

- To instill excitement about a career in business and about the opportunities in such a career to contribute beyond self.

This socializing of students is not the focus or concern of most faculty in American MBA programs. As Harold Leavitt observes, we worry about numbers and types of required courses, about teaching materials, reading assignments, and examinations, about grading standards, about what percentage of our students, no matter how meticulously selected, must receive failing grades.[3] But we spend little time developing consensus on a basic set of attitudes and beliefs—or even discussing what those attitudes and beliefs might be, or what weight their encouragement might be given in the learning experience. We steer clear of the word socialization, for it is "an emotional boobytrap, conjuring up both negative images of mindless obedience and positive visions of collaborative professionalism. The idea of consciously trying to socialize MBA students brings with it a heavy load of ethical and emotional baggage."[4] But, as Leavitt points out, "Whatever our feelings about it, socialization—whether that socialization is intended or inadvertent—is a fact of life in all educational programs, from kindergarten to graduate school."[5] In view of this reality, we who shape the learning experience should accept responsibility for the socialization that occurs during the MBA experience.

Belief 2: *Outstanding leaders, organizations, and practice should be emphasized.*

Too often the press has defined ethics, for itself and the public, as a negative—as misconduct. The recent examples of Ivan Boesky, Jim Bakker, Charles Keating and the Keating Five, and numerous others who have engaged in misrepresentation, deceit, or misdeed in sundry professions, have emphasized the illegal over the ethical. Clearly, misconduct is important, and understanding its systemic causes is a worthwhile pursuit. Without a doubt, compliance systems should be strengthened, and disciplinary action unmistakable in its force and certainty. But if we allow ourselves to become preoccupied with illegal acts, we fail to engage the subject of meaningful leadership, at the very time that such leadership must meet head-on the important issues that today confront our corporations, our country, and the world. Instead, we foster a minimalism that only serves to reduce the significance of these issues by removing them from the broader daily arena of life and work.

A focus on wrongdoing also fuels, by example, a domestic cynicism. It generates a prophecy that, left unchecked, cannot help but be self-fulfilling. Most damaging, it fails to intercept the existing belief structures of the students, who for the most part are quite outstanding. As Parks's study has described (Chapter Two), they are bright, energetic, willing to work hard, and they have a strong sense of interpersonal accountability—of being trustworthy—in immediate face-to-face situations with colleagues and superiors. But many "have only a limited consciousness of systemic harm and injustice, only a limited sense of what is at stake." Often their primary professional value is to achieve success, as defined by the prevailing culture—to do very well materially and to avoid or mask failure. For many, there is an absence of worthy myths and dreams, leaving them vulnerable to unconsidered and inadequate goals, to rationalization of inaction and wrongdoing, to whatever conventional ethos prevails—as long as they are successful within it. They are not yet ready to articulate their values in the service of ethical leadership in public life and to create a positive corporate context.[6]

Ethics and corporate responsibility must be linked to outstanding leaders, organizations, and practice. We must provide interesting and exciting examples if we want to attract and engage students and faculty. A steady diet of cases populated by two-dimensional characters or rife with alleged managerial failure or misconduct falls far short of satisfying this need. What is needed are carefully researched case studies that answer key questions about outstanding business leaders. What challenges did these individuals face? How did they imagine new options? What decisions and actions did they take? What led these individuals to conduct their affairs as they did? What attitudes characterized their organizations? How was corporate and individual purpose defined?[7]

This is not to deny the existence of difficult dilemmas caused by organizational or market failures. Ethics doesn't always pay. But it is important to demonstrate—by rigorous reasoning, not indoctrination—that an active, enlightened concern for ethics and corporate responsibility often is the right path for a firm and for the individual in the long run, economically, organizationally, and competitively. This is the side of ethics education that attracts rather than repels students, faculty, and practitioners. It is a dimension whose relevance is difficult for a professional school and its faculty to deny.

> A great society is a society in which men [women] of business think greatly of their functions.
>
>   Alfred North Whitehead

Belief 3. *The focus should be on decision making with all its complexity and ambiguity, not on issues of ethics or social responsibility in isolation.*

Ethics should contribute to and reflect the decisions and actions of a business enterprise. It must be understood and formulated in ways that are consistent with effective corporate management. To isolate the ethical from the social, the corporate, the competitive, and the economic is to remove it from the very platforms and playing fields most in need of its immediacy. Business and management are thoroughly and undeniably oriented toward practice and action; to distance leadership, ethics, and corporate responsibility from these domains would be to diminish the seriousness with which the discussions proceed, and to encourage posturing. Practitioners do not have the luxury of being concerned solely with the ethical or moral aspects of problems, and—not surprisingly—they find unhelpful those ethical constructs which are far from competitive and organizational realities.

Belief 4. *Immediate intervention is important.*

The decision to initiate ethical discussion on the very first day of the MBA program reflects our strong belief that an immediate grounding and reinforcement are important. The first three to four months of the MBA program are critical, for it is during this time that students struggle hardest to determine whether leadership, ethics, and corporate responsibility have any place in business. Most have standing perceptions, based on interactions with college professors and friends, media reports, and work experiences. They are not confronting ethics for the first time, but they may well be confronting the role of ethics in business for the first time. Too many do so with the preconception that their personal values must be left at the company gate—that their moral lives are one thing, and their business lives are another.

These first three or four months, as noted, are critical. Under severe time pressure, off balance, and eager to fit in, our MBA students watch us very carefully to gauge how central we believe these issues to be to management. It is during these early weeks that our students are most receptive to learning, and their attitudes toward work, performance, and responsibility most subject to influence. This is the instant of standing at the boundary of an organization, of trying to make sense of contradiction and ambiguity, and of being most receptive to cues from the environment. What students learn during this time establishes the track they will go down.[8] If ever our students are open to direction from us, it is during the first months of the program. And if issues of leadership, ethics, and corporate responsibility are not legitimized and addressed effectively during this period, students may well conclude, inaccurately and unfortunately, that such issues are not relevant to the MBA program—or worse, not relevant to business. This latter danger is particularly acute at a school such as Harvard, where the teaching technology is linked so closely to practice and where the classroom discussions are intended to reveal outstanding practice.

The importance of early intervention goes well beyond its immediate impact on the individual. The initial experiences of any team or student group determines, in large part, what happens throughout its existence. Managing the students' first days of membership in an academic community, choosing the impact the institution will have on the expectations and assumptions of those who are joining up: all will have a lasting influence on how the group operates over the long term. One can establish and affirm a sense of joint identity and commitment, or one can abdicate this responsibility—or worse yet, undermine the efforts of those who *do* accept the responsibility. Whatever the choices, the consequences of those moments are significant and enduring.[9]

Finally, positioning ethics at the outset of the first year has positive impacts on other groups. For example, it generates substantial faculty awareness of and interest in the topic and the impact ethics may have on other first-year courses (see Chapter Three).

But early engagement is not without risks and drawbacks. Students are still in the socialization stage—the "joining up" stage—and may be fearful of being perceived as naive. This underscores the importance of the choice and sequencing of topics, not only to minimize the risk of posturing or embarrassment, but also to establish norms of rigorous, realistic reasoning. A second risk is that faculty in other courses may not be prepared to pick up on these issues as they arise in their classes. Finally, some argue that to launch into ethics issues at the outset of the MBA program is necessarily to forego the benefits derived from the depth of knowledge acquired during the first year. This is undoubtedly true; but it does not alter the reality that students arrive with and quickly develop a notion of the abilities, attitudes, and performance that they think are "likely to be applicable and rewarded in an imagined new setting."[10] In any case, this objection could easily be overcome through the addition of a second module either late in the first year or in the second year.

Belief 5. *A broad integrative program is needed.*

The past thirty years have been filled with debate and disagreement as to how best to integrate leadership, ethics, and corporate responsibility into the business school experience. Educators on every level are divided as to whether school systems should attempt to incorporate values into an existing curriculum or establish a new values curriculum. In his comprehensive study of management education for the Carnegie Foundation in 1959, Pierson recommended that a full-year course on the "Places of Business and the Businessman in the Economic, Political, Legal, and Social Environment" be offered in the second year of an MBA program."[11] Gordon and Howell's report, issued the same year, challenged the usefulness of a separate ethics course:

> There is general agreement among business educators that the needed attitudes are not likely to be developed by formal courses in business ethics. . . . There is widespread belief, based as much on hope as on fact, that students are exposed to ethical considerations in most business courses. Probably the schools should give somewhat more explicit consideration to ethical issues and introduce problems having strong ethical overtones into various business courses. We argue, however, that formal courses in business ethics accomplish little and are likely, if anything, to repel the students.[12]

The latter position came under sharp attack in 1974. The Management Division of the Academy of Management's Committee on Curriculum and Standards of the Social Issues argued that unless the social environment were treated in a separate course, instead of receiving pro forma attention in courses devoted to the various functional segments of business, students would not develop an adequate understanding of the business-society relationship. "To permit this subject to be met by being frittered away as a matter of secondary concern in other courses, no matter how well taught, is to distort the perceived significance of the subject matter in the mind of the student," committee members wrote.[13]

The public debate continues, amid growing frustration and discouragement. Lyman Porter and Lawrence McKibbin, in their 1988 report on *Management Education and Development: Drift or Thrust into the 21st Century?*, conclude that

> no reasonable person, in our opinion, could argue that business schools should ignore ethical aspects of business behavior and business decisions or should emphasize them less than currently, but how best to implement an increased emphasis is the challenge. Even more difficult is the question of how to make a concerted focus on ethics in the business curriculum have an impact on graduates' subsequent behavior, to go beyond merely making faculty and students "feel better" because they have discharged their obligations by giving consideration in their courses to moral standards and principles of conduct.[14]

But this debate is flawed on a fundamental level. It poses the approaches as alternatives, rather than mutually reinforcing complements. Experience strongly suggests that the success of a program in leadership, ethics, and corporate responsibility results in part from a sustained discussion of the topic by students and faculty. There is therefore a need to surround the community with multiple opportunities to examine assumptions and beliefs, to challenge ideology, to reformulate purpose—in other words, to ask those questions that education has traditionally accepted as part of its responsibility. Narrow programs that touch a subset of students and a few faculty are valuable but insufficient. Efforts that are short-lived overlook the depth to which old paradigms and old beliefs are etched into the minds of the individuals who collectively constitute the community. The need is for a broad program that includes all three elements: a required course, elective courses, and a purposeful distribution of issues across existing courses in the first year. No single approach has proven to be effective in placing leadership, ethics, and corporate responsibility at the center of the business school experience. Each provides distinctive and important benefits; but implemented in isolation, each has serious shortcomings.

For example, a strategy based on a single required course has many appealing characteristics. First, it is administratively easy, requiring little more than the presence of several ethics specialists, recruited either directly to the faculty or part time from a neighboring philosophy department. Second, issues of ethics and responsibility would be at the very center of the course, rather than an intermittent add-on as is often the case when responsibility is distributed across the faculty. Third, students would be presented with an integrated reasoning process that (if encouraged) might be used in other courses. Fourth, the existence of a required course, staffed by senior faculty, would signal clearly and unambiguously the importance that the institution assigns to these issues. Fifth, a required course, if managed to this end, could provide opportunities for faculty involvement and learning.

Unfortunately, an exclusive reliance on a required course is institutionally and pedagogically misguided. Although a required course early in the first year is very important to the overall effort, there is strong evidence that issues of leadership, ethics, and corporate responsibility must be addressed in all courses. The reasons are twofold. Ethical dilemmas arise in all functional areas and at all levels of the organization. They are embedded in the decisions that managers must make every day. Failing to address these issues when they arise in our courses defines inadequately the responsibilities business school graduates will eventually assume. Second, when we as faculty avoid these issues, we send an unintended but powerful signal that they are not a priority. We inadvertently take an eraser to the good efforts of others. Finally, the refusal to recognize and to address these issues as they arise provides cynics with ammunition for charges of hypocrisy, and—more important—provides students with flawed models of leadership.

What is essential is not necessarily easy. In fact, the integration of leadership, ethics, and corporate responsibility throughout the first-year curriculum may be the single most difficult challenge in assembling a comprehensive program. As Sissela Bok and Daniel Callahan observe in their excellent study, *The Teaching of Ethics in Higher Education,* integration has proven very difficult to attain throughout higher education.[15] In part this stems from the barriers discussed in Chapter Three; in part it results from the failure to provide strong, sustained faculty support; and in part it results from the tendency for broad, overarching, and elusive topics to be inexorably squeezed out of the curriculum by the content of the disciplines in which the faculty are trained. In short, the "hard" drives out the "soft."

The challenges are substantial; but the good news is that they can be met successfully by providing strong, sustained support to the faculty (see Chapter Three); by legitimizing issues of leadership, ethics, and corporate responsibility in a required course, early in the first year; and by surrounding the community with opportunities to discuss these issues. Success does not necessarily require a redesign of courses. In fact, integration throughout the required curriculum can be accomplished effectively through specialization based on specific course domains, the disciplines in which faculty are trained, and the language with which they are most comfortable. In some courses, issues of public policy, regulation, and corporate responsibility are fundamental and accessible. In others, examination of management's responsibility for establishing an organizational context that is consistent with responsible and ethical decisions is key. Still other courses can focus on the individual decision maker faced with a specific ethical dilemma in a particular organizational context. The objective is to create a "virtual" course comprising five-to-six classes in each course for a total of sixty to sixty-five classes throughout the first year. Such a virtual course is inevitably somewhat disjointed. In and of itself, it is insufficient. Nevertheless, it is a critical part of the overall program, in light of the content it transfers and the legitimization it conveys.

Electives are also a valuable component of a broad-based program. They are important by virtue of the numbers of students they can reach and because they represent a source of tested materials for first-year courses and teaching/course development opportunities for faculty for whom these issues are a central focus. Elective courses provide faculty members with a chance to focus on a particular aspect of leadership, ethics, and corporate responsibility and thereby achieve greater depth of understanding.

However, a program that relies primarily on electives is insufficient in two ways. First, only a small percentage of students take a particular elective, and those who do are not necessarily those to whom the elective offers the greatest potential benefit. Second, because electives are usually offered later in a student's course of study, their impacts on community norms and individual learning are usually limited. Again, these are *not* arguments for abandoning electives. To the contrary, these strengths and weaknesses suggest the importance of building electives into a broad, integrated program that also includes a required course early in the first year and integration throughout the first-year curriculum. As noted previously, each of these elements in isolation has serious deficiencies (summarized in Figure 4.1), but these negatives can be neutralized when the three approaches are viewed as complementary.

Belief 6. *Surround the community with opportunities to discuss leadership, ethics, and corporate responsibility.*

An effective program needs to surround the community with opportunities to discuss leadership, ethics, and corporate

Figure 4.1
Neutralization of Potential Negatives

REQUIRED COURSE

Strengths	*Potential Negatives*	*Neutralization*
1. Administratively easy	1. Seen as "the ethics course"	1. Encourage discussion of leadership, ethics, and corporate responsibility in all first-year courses
2. Ensures focus	2. Failure to discuss issues as they arise across all courses feeds cynicism, takes an eraser to the work of others, and provides a flawed model of responsible leadership	
3. Careful teaching of reasoning process		
4. Strong signal from administration		
5. Energizes student interest		
6. Faculty learning opportunity		

ELECTIVE COURSES

Strengths	*Potential Negatives*	*Neutralization*
1. Opportunity for advanced study	1. Many students do not take the electives	1. Include a required course on leadership, ethics, and corporate responsibility at the outset of MBA program
2. Source of tested material for use in first-year required course	2. Because they are usually taken late in the program, electives have limited impact	2. Integrate discussion of ethics issues into all first-year courses
3. Opportunity for specialized teaching, research, and course development		

DISTRIBUTION ACROSS EXISTING COURSES

Strengths	*Potential Negatives*	*Neutralization*
1. Demonstrates that dilemmas and questions are not isolated problems, but present throughout the organization	1. Fragmented teaching yields fragmented understanding of the issues and reasoning process	1. Include a required course on leadership, ethics, and corporate responsibility at the outset of MBA program
2. Strong legitimization by faculty	2. Without strong student interest, treatment of these topics by many faculty tends to be intermittent	
3. Integrates a concern for leadership, ethics, and corporate responsibility into the managerial decision-making process		

responsibility. Required and elective courses are obvious elements, but the MBA experience is clearly much broader than courses and classes. Opportunities to influence agendas, to signal what the community believes to be the core of management, abound. What questions are asked on the MBA application form and in admissions interviews? What type of experiences and characteristics seem to be valued in the selection process? What is discussed at the orientation program for new students? Whom does the school invite as eminent speakers? What institutional support is provided for community outreach programs, for nonprofit summer internships, for field studies of nonprofit organizations, for a student-edited business ethics journal? In part the goal is to contribute to the immediate well-being of the community; but even more important is awakening students to the multitude of opportunities to contribute over a lifetime.

Belief 7. *Faculty encouragement and development are as important as student development, at least during the first five to seven years.*

The teaching of leadership, ethics, and corporate responsibility needs to be a concern of the faculty at large, not the domain of a few specialists. All must support the program, and many must actively participate in it. In part, this belief reflects the very magnitude of the challenge, and the effort necessary to meet that challenge. But it also reflects an educational reality: that all teachers carry the eraser referred to earlier. When we decide not to talk about leadership, ethics, and corporate responsibility, we undermine the progress that other people have made in this critical area.

The implications are clear: the structure of a program on leadership, ethics, and corporate responsibility must be designed with close attention to faculty encouragement, development, and participation. Opportunities must be created for more of us to become familiar with student reactions to ethics and corporate responsibility, to broaden faculty interest and awareness, to understand the perceived ethical dimensions of our theories and analytics and of our teaching and mentoring methods, to explore our own belief structure, and to understand the often inadvertent signals that we send.[16]

Belief 8. *Strong, visible commitment by the dean and senior faculty leaders is essential.*

Concern for leadership, ethics, and corporate responsibility runs counter to the recent priorities of management education and the values it espouses. This conflict is perhaps not surprising. It should be remembered that as recently as thirty years ago American schools of business were troubled institutions. Two major studies, cited earlier, produced substantial volumes confirming that academic quality was uneven and generally too low. The 1959 Ford Foundation study, for example, found

> strong and widespread dissatisfaction with the quality of business education in American colleges and universities today. What passes as the going standard of acceptability among business schools is embarrassingly low, and many schools of business do not meet even these low standards. While the schools are still bedeviled by uncertainty, there is growing recognition that the present situation is intolerable.[17]

Most research conducted by the business schools, the report observed,

> attempts merely to describe current practice, or going a short step further to develop normative rules which summarize what is considered to be the best of prevailing practice. The business literature is not, in general, characterized by challenging hypothesis, well-developed conceptual frameworks, the use of sophisticated research techniques, penetrating analysis, the use of evidence drawn from the relevant underlying disciplines—or very significant conclusions.[18]

Business education was judged to be adrift, "a restless and uncertain giant in the halls of higher education . . . gnawed by doubt and harassed by barbs of unfriendly critics," according to the report.

> It seeks to serve several masters and is assured by its critics that it serves none well. . . . [Schools of business administration] search for academic respectability, while most of them continue to engage in unrespectable vocational training. They seek to be professional schools, while expressing doubt themselves that the occupation

for which they prepare students can rightfully be called a profession.[19]

In the Carnegie Corporation's report also issued in 1959, author Pierson commented, "On a number of counts, the general quality of work done at business schools and other institutions in the business area appears sorely deficient."[20]

Although these reports did raise questions of the proper content and scope of business education, their strongest call—or the call heard most strongly—was for higher standards, systematic knowledge, research more analytical then descriptive, and a more scientific attitude toward management problems. A new and better basis for professional competence had to be found. The analytical method, more than any other tool, was seized on as the most powerful and reliable means of dealing with a wide range of business problems in all areas.

The call for a scientific approach was not surprising. Observed Donald Schon in *Educating the Reflective Practitioner:*

> The professional schools of the modern research university are premised on technical rationality. Their normative curriculum, first adopted in the early decades of the twentieth century as the professions sought to gain prestige by establishing their schools in universities, still embodies the idea that practical competence becomes professional when its instrumental problemsolving is grounded in systematic, preferably scientific knowledge. . . . The greater one's proximity to basic science, as a rule, the higher one's academic status.[21]

Thus the Ford Foundation and Carnegie Corporation reports, in tandem with the wider academic trends described by Schon, shaped what would be valued in management education for the next thirty years. Emphasis shifted to that which was known, quantifiable, and demonstrable. Even the choice of decisions and individual transactions to be studied was influenced by their susceptibility to the scientific method and newly developed analytics.

Of course, none of these authorities argued against a consideration of the broader purpose of business within society. None actively minimized the importance of the decisions of individual managers and the policies of individual firms in the quality of collective and individual lives, or the need for managers to reflect and act on that awareness. But they did change the priorities of business education. By identifying certain deficiencies in business education—real deficiencies, which threatened the field's standing within both the university and practice—and by focusing energy and attention on these issues, they effectively relegated other dimensions of business education to the periphery.

Strong sustained commitment will be required of deans and senior faculty leaders if management education is to strike an appropriate balance among knowledge, skills, and values (see Figure 4.2). The initial implications for faculty attempting to mount a broad program of leadership, ethics, and corporate responsibility, and to integrate that program into the ethos and mission of a school, are substantial. (See Chapter Three.) We should always remember that many faculty are already fully consumed by their established challenges: understanding practice, achieving teaching excellence, developing teaching materials, and conducting academically respectable research. This is particularly true for those faculty who are highly trained in a discipline, but who have little work experience or classroom exposure to management. The integration of leadership, ethics, and corporate responsibility into their courses moves such faculty away from their proven areas of expertise and may put them at risk of being branded as "soft" or naive by a community cynical about business, authority, and organization.

Other challenges abound. The academic reward system, for example, offers little incentive to faculty to join what is easily perceived to be a risky venture. Promotion and tenure decisions may fail to take account of a faculty member's decision to address issues of leadership, ethics, and corporate responsibility. Of course, standards must be maintained, and mediocre

Figure 4.2
Rebalancing Learning Objectives

ATTITUDES . . .
  BELIEFS
"Purpose" . . . Vision
Courage, Integrity
Trusting, Supportive
Accountable
Change-Oriented
Stakeholder-Focused
Team Player
Action-Oriented
Global Perspective
Learning-Oriented
Empathy

KNOWLEDGE   CRITICAL SKILLS
Global . . . Interna-   Communication
  tional   Leadership
External Environment   Broad Perspective
Cross-Cultural   People Management
Technology   Management
Customer and Market   —Problem/Opportu-
New Organizational   nity ID
  Forms   —Analytical
Total Quality Manage-   —Information pro-
  ment   cessing
Cross-Functional   —Decision making
Functional   —Planning
Industry Specific   —Implementation

work must not be rewarded simply because a field is deemed to be important. But our signals are extremely important. It is striking that a clear failure to extend research, course development, and teaching, where appropriate, into the domain of ethics, corporate responsibility, and public policy is seldom even noticed when tenure-granting or recruiting decisions are made.

These are serious matters for any dean; and they arise at a time when, according to McKibbin and Porter, there is no forceful push for curricular change emanating from the business schools themselves.[22] This is in part because the strategy followed by business schools over the past thirty years has been highly successful in addressing many of the criticisms stated in the Ford Foundation and Carnegie Corporation reports. Business school faculties, with rare exception, are no longer objects of derision, either within the university or from the business community.[23] Business school research has ceased to be the target it once was and deserved to be.[24] The curriculum is comfortably aligned with the belief structures, competencies, and priorities of the faculty that designed it—although we should note that this is a group selected in response to the criticisms and concerns of more than thirty years ago.

There are other important evidences of a successful strategy. As shown in Table 4.1, the number of students studying business has increased dramatically, creating opportunities for faculty and revenues for the university.

And, in marked contrast to the reports issued in the 1950s, researchers did not identify any great disenchantment with either the BBA or MBA degrees as preparation for careers in the world of business and management.[25] In fact, a mastery of analytics has proven to be the passport to the highest paying—and, for many students the most attractive—positions in business.

It is the very success of an old strategy in meeting old challenges that is one of the greatest barriers to the integration of

Table 4.1 Degrees in Business Administration in the United States

	BBA Degrees		MBA Degrees	
	Total	% of All BAs	Total	% of All Masters
1962–63	54,000	13.1%	6,000	6.3%
1972–73	128,000	13.8	31,000	11.8
1982–83	227,000	23.4	65,000	22.5
1988–89	238,000	23.4	73,000	23.5

Source: National Center for Education Statistics.

leadership, ethics, and corporate responsibility into the center of management education today.

Program Structure

Decision Making and Ethical Values Module

For the past four years, the opening sessions of the Harvard Business School's MBA program have been dedicated to a required module: Decision Making and Ethical Values: An Introduction. This module has six specific aims and objectives. First, it discusses the breadth of responsibility of the modern corporation and the constraints and trade-offs that attend the exercise of that responsibility. Second, it emphasizes the centrality of ethical values in the context of individual and organizational effectiveness. Third, it demonstrates the dangers of ignoring the impact of business decisions and strategies on the full range of stakeholders; indeed, it encourages the incorporation of ethical values and stakeholder analysis in the broadest range of business decision making. Fourth, it encourages respect for law. Fifth, it provides a process for evaluating the economic and noneconomic consequences of proposed decisions, strategies, and implementation plans. Sixth, and most important, the module signals the centrality of these issues, legitimizes their discussion, and creates the expectation that matters of leadership, ethics, and corporate responsibility will be discussed as they arise throughout the existing program.

The first part of the nine-session module examines the ways in which the purposes of corporations and the responsibilities of managers are shaped by political, economic, and social systems. Next to be examined are leadership issues, particularly as they relate to human relationships and the ethical climate that managers create within corporations. Finally, we pose basic questions to students about personal integrity and the work of management: specifically, about how managers can best relate life values and commitment to work-related responsibilities and ambitions, and how they can develop the creativity and personal courage needed to manage ethically and successfully (see Figure 4.3). As Kenneth Andrews has phrased it:

> Ethical decisions require three qualities that cannot be impossible to find and develop. These are, first, the ability to recognize ethical issues and to think through the consequences of alternative resolutions. Second is the self-confidence to seek out different points of view and then decide what is right at a given time and place in a particular set of relationships and combination of circumstances. Third is what William James called tough-mindedness, which in this case is the willingness to make decisions when all that needs to be known cannot be known and the questions that press for answers have no established and incontrovertible solutions. [26]

The module is purposely short for several reasons. First, a module of only nine classes cannot be described as "*the* ethics course" by faculty teaching in existing courses. Instead, the module is acknowledged to be an introduction to a set of issues to be discussed further in other first-year courses—no more, no less. Second, the brevity of the module makes it possible to attract to the teaching group highly visible senior faculty from each area, thereby ensuring strong teaching, diverse perspectives, and broad ownership. It has made it feasible to invite

Figure 4.3 Decision Making and Ethical Values: An Introduction

Module Organization and Themes

Sessions 1, 2 and 3 — Ethics and the Corporation

The power and responsibility of the modern corporation. The limitations of two principal surrogates for ethics: the market and the law.

Sessions 4, 5 and 6 — Ethics, Organizational Context, and the Individual

The key role of leadership as a bridge between individual and organizational values. Ethical values in domestic and global business enterprises. Organizational pressures toward and away from personal moral integrity.

Sessions 7, 8 and 9 — Ethics and the Individual

Determinants of moral awareness. The analytics of specific ethical dilemmas. Effectiveness in raising ethical concerns.

two other first-year teaching groups to audit the module each year, allowing them to gain familiarity with the materials and to observe directly classroom dynamics—the broad involvement of the students, the seriousness with which they reason through issues, and the teaching strategies of the module faculty.

Student-written evaluations of the ethics module have been consistently high since its introduction in 1988 (see Table 4.2). The results of questionnaire surveys administered to all first-year students on completion of the module are consistent with the tenor of focus-group discussion and individual student interviews, and with the observations offered by class auditors during the four years the module has been part of the required curriculum. Perhaps most important, the faculty who have taught the module uniformly describe the experience as one of the most satisfying and stimulating teaching experiences during their careers. This experience confirms that senior faculty from across the school can teach the required module effectively and with great enjoyment and satisfaction, despite limited training in "ethics" as a formal discipline.

Integration Across the First-Year Curriculum

Substantial progress has been made in integrating leadership, ethics, and corporate responsibility into a number of first-year courses.[27] Although there has been an ethics component in the required curriculum in the past—actively discussed in some courses, intermittently addressed in others, and only latent in others—there is a distinct difference today. In the past few years, an aggressive case-development initiative and strong course leadership has resulted in more cases with explicit ethical content. "What is different in the last few years," explains Professor William Bruns, course head for Financial Reporting and Management Accounting, "is that the required module has raised student awareness of ethics issues. Where once we might have approached a financial reporting case by focusing exclusively on the financial issues, today students are more

Table 4.2 Student-Written Evaluations of Decision Making and
Ethical Values: Averages for the years 1988, 1989, and
1990

Module Objective	Level of Effectiveness in Meeting the Objective (1 = ineffective; 5 very effective)
Recognition of the centrality of ethical values in the context of individual and organizational effectiveness	4.5
Recognition of the dangers of ignoring the impact of business decisions on the full range of stakeholders	4.4
Recognition of the breadth of responsibility of the modern corporation, as well as the constraints and trade-offs attending the exercise of that responsibility	4.4
Recognition of the importance of incorporating stakeholder analysis and ethical values throughout business decision making	4.4
Respect for law and regulation, as well as an awareness of their limitations	4.1
Development of a process for reasoning through the economic and noneconomic consequences of proposed strategies and implementation plans	4.0
Encouragement of reflection on the value and constraints in the students own approach to ethical reasoning	4.7

likely to discern and discuss the ethics of alternative reporting approaches. What it comes down to is that today, we walk with, not away from, ethics issues."

The progress results in part from a strategy designed to include four to six ethics-related classes in each of ten first-year courses, which has proven to be a reasonable and attainable goal. It results, too, from the provision of strong support to faculty (see Chapter Three). But the most important success factor was the courage and strong leadership of several course heads and their teaching groups. The Marketing course is a

ars ago," observes course head
eaching group decided to take
e cases that raise ethical issues.
Marketing modules, we have
s, not exclusively, but promi-
t surprisingly, the Organiza-
esource Management courses
fertile area for developing eth-
se head Professor Louis B.
cal issues to run the gamut of
o involve important aspects of
he issues." The courses address
r can live up to personal values
, the management of a diverse
organizational context on con-

rred in how ethical considera-
on, Organization and Control.
head and faculty chair of the
the strategy in that area is to
nd then follow and highlight
out the course." He cites pri-
rmation systems on behavior,
relevant.

gress in integrating ethics into
Technology and Operations

UNIVERSITY OF ST FRANCIS

MOSER PERFORMING ARTS CENTER AUDITORIUM

Featured Speaker: Valerie Martin

SATURDAY, MARCH 20 - 9 A.M.

ENGLISH LANGUAGE AND LITERATURE

UNDERGRADUATE CONFERENCE ON

13TH ANNUAL

Management (TOM) course. Course head Steven Wheelwright and his colleagues decided to try to identify and address the ethical issues that manufacturing managers were
most likely to come up against. As a result, the course today
includes work-force issues of equity, safety, lay-offs, and several cases focused on the environment. Although TOM also
includes a number of older cases with implicit ethical issues
that are now receiving greater attention than before, Wheelwright points to an inherent difference in the cases being developed today. "In our newer cases, as in the workplace, ethical issues and operations issues are inextricable," he explains.
"The approach of subdividing a situation and dealing with one
issue at a time isn't appropriate with ethics issues. It's important that we see these as integral with operations issues and
examine them all at once. We're still learning how to do that,"
he continues, "but we do know that we have to avoid having a
'time out for ethics' at the end of a discussion. We have to find
ways to teach that integrate ethics considerations at every
point at which they are relevant."

This spirit—embraced by all of the first-year course heads,
albeit in differing ways and to a varying extent—has been a
significant contributor to the program.

Second-Year Electives

The school's emphasis on ethics in the first-year curriculum is
reinforced in a variety of second-year electives. Some were explicitly conceived as part of the Leadership, Ethics, and Corporate Responsibility initiative: The Business World—Moral
and Social Inquiry Through Fiction; Moral Dilemmas of
Management; Managing Information in a Competitive Context—Ethical and Legal Perspectives; and Profits, Markets and
Values.

The Business World—Moral and Social Inquiry Through
Fiction exposes students to literary observers of commercial
enterprise as a way of considering the ethical and existential
aspects of life and work.[28] Fiction is employed as an instrument

of social and cultural observation and a source of moral energy. The novels discussed afford a close look at aspects of business life, the setting and pursuit of life and career goals, and the interdependence of personal, family, and professional life. The "lens" with which this course hopes to equip students is that of self-reflection and self-inquiry through metaphor. Through short stories, plays, and novels by people including Tolstoy, F. Scott Fitzgerald, Arthur Miller, Saul Bellow, Walker Percy, and Gloria Naylor, students encounter a number of themes at the core of personal and professional experience: success and failure, free will and obligation, goal setting, commitment, and making decisions at life's turning points.

Moral Dilemmas of Management attempts to impart an appreciation for the enormous power and attendant responsibilities that accrue to business executives in modern industrial societies. The moral, legal, and economic obligations of these executives sometimes come into conflict, giving rise to potentially destructive dilemmas. The course draws on the works and ideas of philosophers, economists, historians, and others to build a framework for analyzing and identifying practical responsible solutions to these dilemmas, which constitute critical episodes in the lives of individuals and the management of companies.

Managing Information in a Competitive Context—Ethical and Legal Perspectives employs cases that present difficult decisions facing managers, courts, policy makers, and industry groups, in order to explore tensions among the multiple purposes information serves. The course's principal educational objectives are (1) to prepare students to formulate and defend decisions relating to the acquisition, use, protection, and dissemination of information, (2) to equip students for leadership roles in shaping and implementing norms of business conduct, and (3) to expose students to the perspectives of other professionals with whom they will be working and negotiating throughout their careers. It also provides Harvard Business School students, whose classmates in this case include Harvard

Law School and Kennedy School of Government students, an unusual exposure to the perspectives and belief structures of lawyers and government officials.

Profits, Markets and Values is designed to provide students with conceptual frameworks for anticipating social concerns about business, developing strategies to deal with these concerns, and constructively integrating social values into sound business decision making. The frameworks combine a recognition of the economic realities of business life with a broader social perspective. The course is also designed to provide an opportunity for students to formulate their own views about the purpose of business, the appropriate norms of business practice, and the strengths and weaknesses of markets in providing for the common good.

Of course, ethical study in the second-year curriculum is not restricted to these four courses. The examination of moral dilemmas and the exploration of personal and corporate responsibility are significant issues in several other ethics-related electives, including The Coming of Managerial Capitalism, Comparative Business-Government Relations, Law and the Corporate Manager, Power and Influence, and Self-Assessment and Career Development.

The Coming of Managerial Capitalism emphasizes an understanding of the historical development of modern business practices and policies, examination of nonbusiness institutions such as labor unions and government regulatory and legislative bodies that have an impact on business activities, and awareness of changing American attitudes and values and their impact on the environment in which managers must work. Comparative Business-Government Relations attempts to impart an understanding of the roles and relationships of business and government in key countries of Asia, Europe, and the Americas, of how and why these roles and relationships are changing, and of what choices these changes have opened up for managers. Power and Influence explores the duties, responsibilities, and obligations that accompany the rights and privileges of influential positions. The perspective of the course is that of early to mid-career manager, and the focus is on the challenges of everyday managerial life.

Ethical issues are also raised in Law and the Corporate Manager. The issues discussed in this course are ones that the public perceives to be at the core of business ethics: insider trading and proxy rules, antitrust issues, fiduciary obligations, compliance with federal antifraud regulations, compensation and pension arrangements, and corporate governance. Taking this course, students gain a better awareness of the line between ethical decisions that are merely a matter of legal compliance, and those in the difficult gray areas, beyond the letter of the law.

The ethics electives, like the first-year module, are well received by the students. On an educational importance scale of 1 (low) to 5 (high), these courses are typically rated from 4.3 to 4.9. Another sign of their effectiveness is the enrollment statistics, as shown in Table 4.3.

Community Outreach

Many schools have introduced community outreach programs in recent years in the conviction that community service is an integral responsibility of leadership and that their students should cultivate a habit of service. Harvard Business School is no exception. Hundreds of Harvard Business School students become involved every year in community outreach efforts and projects. The Harvard Community Volunteer Association, which serves as a clearinghouse for and sponsor of volunteer opportunities and activities in the Boston and Cambridge areas, facilitates students' involvement in such projects and programs as clothing, food, and blood drives; meal preparation at local soup kitchens; math and reading tutoring at local Boys' and Girls' Clubs; and English-language tutoring. The student-initiated Project Outreach annually brings Harvard students, faculty, and staff together to work jointly on designated community service projects. The school's Eminent

Table 4.3   Enrollment Statistics for Ethics-Related Elective Courses

	Enrollment in Courses Academic Year 1991–1992[a]
Power and Influence	219
Moral Dilemmas of Management	168
The Business World: Moral and Social Inquiry Through Fiction	75
Comparative Business- Government Relations	41
The Coming of Managerial Capitalism	379
Law and the Corporate Manager	79
Managing Information in a Competitive Context: Ethical and Legal Perspectives	30
Self-Assessment and Career Development	57

[a]Electives are open only to second-year students; the second-year class numbers 800.

Speakers Program brings outstanding political, business, and civic leaders to campus. The institution's commitment to service is further underscored by an education partnership, through which the school is helping the William Howard Taft Middle School in Brighton, Massachusetts, meet broad educational objectives for its students. Student commitment is also evident in the student-edited *Business Ethics Forum,* a vehicle for encouraging thoughtful reflection on issues and matters of ethics through the publication of relevant interviews, essays, and case studies.

The evidence is clear: our students are not the problem. Almost all of them are eager to talk about purpose and principle, to explore the systemic causes and consequences of unethical behavior, to study outstanding leaders and organizations as they grapple with ethical dilemmas, and to identify opportunities to contribute to the larger community. The problem rests with the failure of education to encourage and assist students in their search for purpose and worth.

APPENDIX I

Business Ethics and the Harvard Business School

Until recently the history of business ethics and the Harvard Business School* has mirrored that of management education: voiced commitment, limited experimentation, and repeated disappointments.

In 1907, with the character of the school still very much on the drawing boards, Professor A. Lawrence Lowell—soon to become president of Harvard—pushed quickly beyond the question of whether to include ethics in the curriculum to that of how to do so. Lowell was quite explicit on this point, arguing not for a required course on business ethics, but for the subject's distribution across the curriculum. "The way to inculcate good morals," he argued, "is not so much formal preaching as letting them appear as an integral part of the principles that are explained or demonstrated."

Dean Edwin F. Gay, whose views were initially consistent with Lowell's, concluded in 1917 that ethics education should be incorporated specifically in the required Business Policy course. His successor, Wallace B. Donham, in a 1922 report to Harvard president Lowell, noted that instruction in business ethics was much on the minds of his faculty, and that the professionalization of business demanded a collection of cases on the subject and adequate classroom instruction to give it

* Based on Jeffrey L. Cruikshank, *A Delicate Experiment* (Boston: Harvard Business School Press, 1987).

151

proper emphasis. Carl F. Taeusch, who held a doctorate in philosophy from Harvard, was subsequently hired from the State University of Iowa to conduct the first formal experiment in the teaching of business ethics as an elective course. "Although moral fiber can scarcely be created in the student," Donham wrote in a 1929 report to Lowell, "the more common ethical dilemmas of business can be presented to him while he has time for deliberate consideration free from the pressure of circumstance." But Taeusch's course, more theoretical than practical, never won sufficient student support, and—despite Donham's strong advocacy for it—was discontinued in 1935. Taeusch's effort, and another in the mid-1930s, seem to have dampened the desire to tackle the subject at all.

With the end of World War II, the school resumed educating civilians, and renewed its experimentation with how best to address issues of business ethics and corporate responsibility in the curriculum. A required course on Public Relationships and Responsibilities (1946–1948) was succeeded by a required course on Business Responsibilities in the American Society (1949–1960), which in turn was replaced by The Manager and the American Economy (1961–1963), Planning in the Business Environment (1963–1972), Environmental Analysis for Managers (1972–1978), and Business, Government, and the International Economy (1979–present). These latter courses, reflecting faculty interests, focused increasingly on political economy and regulation.

In 1963, corporate social responsibility as a topic was transferred formally to Business Policy, a required course that met three times a week throughout the second year of the MBA program. The controlling concept of corporate strategy was enlarged to include personal values and obligations to society in the formulation of strategy. However, as Business Policy evolved into Competition and Strategy in the first year, the perspective on strategy formulation focused primarily on economic considerations.

By the mid-1980s, the Harvard Business School had returned to a strategy based on several ethics-related electives in the second year. Debate as to how these issues might best be addressed—in a required ethics course, in elective ethics courses, or throughout the curriculum—had subsided, despite the outstanding individual contributions and commitments of several faculty, including Professors Andrews, Arthur, Goodpaster, Matthews, Nash, and Toffler. Each approach had fallen short of the institutional sense of responsibility; each dean had shared Dunham's disappointment that "desire outruns performance all along the line"; and the attention of most faculty was focused on other important challenges.

APPENDIX II

Listing of Internal Research Projects*

1. "An Overview of the Field of Business Ethics and Corporate Social Responsibility"—Kimerer LaMothe and Audrey Sullivan Jacob
   • Based on a review of more than one hundred articles, books, and conference papers, the report summarizes the current literature and outlines basic conceptual framework.
2. "Ethics in Business: Individual Characteristics and Corporate Context"—Kimerer LaMothe and Audrey Sullivan Jacob
   • Based on a review of the business ethics and business leadership literature, the report highlights individual characteristics, including personal attributes and knowledge, which scholars often cite as prerequisites for ethical managers and leaders. The report also describes the components of a corporate context which can foster ethical behavior by employees.
3. "Imaging the Field of Ethics"—Kimerer LaMothe
   • Based on earlier reports, the report provides a visual image of the main topic areas or aspects of the business ethics field and outlines the dif-

* The internal research projects are listed in the chronological order in which the research was done.

fering approaches taken to business ethics by
moral philosophy, theology, and business ethics. A later supplement to the report identified
the most important discipline underlying each
aspect.

4. Teaching and Research Initiatives in Business Ethics at
   Leading American Business Schools—Audrey Sullivan
   Jacob
   - Based on four months of travel to major busi-
     ness schools, the report describes courses and
     activities in professional ethics at eight schools.
     The report provides a relatively comprehensive
     sample of pedagogical methods and programs
     in business ethics education, and outlines gen-
     eral barriers to the incorporation of ethical is-
     sues in the curricula of business schools.

5. "Ethical Content in the First-Year Curriculum"—
   Mary McGovern
   - Based on interviews with teaching faculty
     members, the report highlights the materials in
     each functional course that raise ethical con-
     cerns, outlines factors that affect ethical discus-
     sions, and proposes areas for development of
     ethical considerations in the curriculum.

6. "Report on the Barriers to the Integration of Ethics
   into the First-Year Curriculum and on Faculty Development Needs"—Mary Gentile
   - Based on extensive conversations with faculty
     members, the report identifies specific barriers
     and proposes a number of alternative opportu-
     nities for faculty support that will improve the
     coverage of ethical and social concerns in MBA
     courses.

7. "The Development of Section E: 1986–87"—Margaret
   McKenna
   - This study is based on personal observations of

Section E in the classroom and at social events, and traces the development of the section.

8. "Integrating Ethics into the Harvard Business School Classroom: Current Dynamics and Future Trends"— Rachel Hoffman
   • Based on observation of forty-seven first-year Marketing classes in two sections, the report describes conflicting influences on the classroom agenda, emphasizing the impact of this on value-based discussions, and on faculty and students' perceptions of ethics.

9. "Observations on Value-Based Discussions in the Production and Operations Management Course"—Piper Orton
   • Based on observations of POM courses, the report summarizes the frequency with which latent value issues are present in classroom discussions, and the reasons why these issues tend to receive inadequate attention.

10. "Integration Research: The Layer Cake Model (1987–88)"—Kimerer LaMothe and Audrey Sullivan Jacob
    • This work tightens the description of the topics that collectively constitute the field of business ethics and corporate responsibility, provides a list of dominant disciplines helpful in addressing issues within each topic, and outlines teaching objectives for each topic area.

11. "Teaching Ethics in Law School,"—Audrey Sullivan Jacob
    • The report is based on information on legal ethics programs at leading American law schools and on extensive library research. It contains a brief history of legal education and the development of training in legal ethics, summarizes two conferences on the teaching of legal ethics or professional responsibility, describes current

methods for teaching ethics in law schools, and
lists parallels to management education.

12. "The Challenge of Ethical Discussions in the MBA
Classroom: Student Assumptions and Faculty Paradigms"—Mary Gentile

• Based on extensive observation of classes in the
financial reporting and management accounting
course, this report identifies student assumptions and the conceptual paradigms that stifle
the integration of ethical analysis into the discussion, and provides some suggestions on how
these barriers might be overcome.

NOTES

1. Harold J. Leavitt, "Educating Our MBAs: On Teaching What We
Haven't Taught," *California Management Review* (Spring 1980),
p. 40.

2. A number of schools are developing broad-based programs
aimed at integrating ethics and corporate responsibility into their
MBA programs. The excellent program under way at Wharton
is described in Thomas W. Dunfee and Diana C. Robertson, "Integrating Ethics into the Business School Curriculum," *Journal of
Business Ethics* (November 1988), pp. 847–860. Programs of similar breadth but somewhat different design are also well under
way at a number of other schools, including (to name only a few)
the University of Virginia's Darden School, Georgetown, and
Notre Dame.

3. Harold J. Leavitt, "Socializing Our MBAs: Total Immersion?
Managed Culture? Brainwashing?," *Selections* (Winter 1991), p. 4.

4. Ibid.

5. Ibid.

6. This description of student belief structures is based on the research of Sharon Parks, as reported in Chapter Two, p. 19ff.

7. Harvard Professor Richard Tedlow has commenced a major,
multiyear research program on corporate leaders who have em-
bodied ethical corporate leadership. Stanford Professor Kirk
Hanson and the Business Enterprise Trust have instituted an
annual awards program for individuals at all levels of the orga-

nization who demonstrate through their actions a strong sense of ethics.

8. David E. Berlew and Douglas T. Hall, "The Socialization of Managers: Effects of Expectations on Performance," *Administrative Science Quarterly* 11, 2 (September 1966), p. 210.

9. J. Richard Hackman, "Group-Level Issues in the Design and Training of Cockpit Crews," in H. H. Orlady and H. C. Fowshee, eds., *Proceedings of the NASA/MAC Workshop on Cockpit Resource Management* (Moffett Field, CA: NASA-Ames Research Center, 1986), pp. 29–31.

10. John Van Maanen, "Golden Passports: Managerial, Socialization and Graduate Education," *The Review of Higher Education* 6, 4 (Summer 1983), p. 436.

11. Frank C. Pierson et al., *The Education of American Businessmen: A Study of University-College Programs in Business Administration* (New York: McGraw-Hill, 1959), p. 92.

12. Robert A. Gordon and James E. Howell, *Higher Education for Business* (New York: Columbia University Press, 1959), p. 111.

13. Charles W. Powers and David Vogel, *Ethics in the Education of Business Managers* (Briarcliff Manor, NY: The Hastings Center, 1980), pp. 27–28.

14. Lyman W. Porter and Lawrence E. McKibbin, *Management Education and Development: Drift or Thrust into the 21st Century?* (New York: McGraw-Hill, 1988), p. 86.

15. Sissela Bok and Daniel Callahan, *The Teaching of Ethics in Higher Education* (Briarcliff Manor, NY: The Hastings Center, 1980), pp. 74–75.

16. Mary Gentile, "The Challenge of Ethical Discussions in the MBA Classroom: Student Assumptions and Faculty Paradigms," Harvard Business School working paper, 1992.

17. Gordon and Howell, *Higher Education for Business*, p. 6.

18. Ibid., p. 379.

19. Ibid., pp. 4–5.

20. Pierson et al., *The Education of American Businessmen*, p. xvi.

21. Donald A. Schon, *Educating the Reflective Practitioner* (San Francisco and London: Jossey-Bass, 1987), pp. 8–9.

22. Porter and McKibbin, *Management Education and Development*, p. 80.

23. Ibid., p. 147.

24. Ibid., p. 179.
25. Ibid., p. 86.
26. Kenneth R. Andrews, ed., *Ethics in Practice: Managing the Moral Corporation* (Boston: Harvard Business School Press, 1989), p. 6.
27. Discussion of the integration of leadership, ethics, and corporate responsibility into the first-year course is based heavily on Deborah Blagg, Garry Emmons, Nancy Perry, and John Simon, "Ethics in the MBA Curriculum (Part I)," *HBS Bulletin* (December 1991), pp. 42–52.
28. Description of the second-year elective, The Business World—Moral and Social Inquiry Through Fiction, draws from Pamela Troyer, "Ethics in the MBA Curriculum (Part II)," *HBS Bulletin* (February 1992), pp. 26–33.

CHAPTER FIVE

Epilogue

THOMAS R. PIPER

The accomplishments of the initiative in Leadership, Ethics, and Corporate Responsibility during the past five years have been substantial. Those involved in the effort have achieved the needed consensus, at the requisite level, to undertake the challenging task; they have developed a strategy for its pursuit; they have generated support among faculty; and they have effected its implementation. A required course has been introduced; four new electives have been added; course heads have begun to integrate new issues of ethics and corporate responsibility into the first-year curriculum; and a large percentage of our students have enriched the life of our community, and their own lives, through public service.

It would be premature, however, to claim victory, or to assume that these accomplishments are now and henceforth safely institutionalized. The five-year period just completed, devoted to the introduction and expansion of the program, have in some ways been the "easy" years because of the excitement and novelty of the initiative and the supportive context of a heightened societal concern. History suggests that sustaining such a program will be even more challenging than launching it. There is in the nature of educational institutions a set of circumstances that can work against the perpetuation of any initiative: the rapid turnover of faculty and leadership; the continuous flow of new ideas and major themes that vie for faculty attention and institutional resources; the tendency, mentioned in earlier chapters, for the "hard" to drive out the "soft"; the excessively full agendas of those relatively new to teaching, who—fresh from doctoral programs into which these issues have not yet been integrated—must now demonstrate an ethical awareness at the same time they are developing strong teaching skills, devising and executing fruitful research projects, and cultivating an international managerial perspective.

Furthermore, the challenges before the program in Leadership, Ethics, and Corporate Responsibility are even greater than those faced by most academic endeavors. These issues are so fundamental to effective leadership and so pervasive throughout organizations (and therefore throughout our courses) that the great majority of the faculty must support the initiative if it is to succeed fully. That level of support is difficult to attain. While it is true that our efforts have benefited from a heightened public concern about the excesses and ethical failings that were so visible in the 1980s, it seems that this concern does not yet go deep enough.

A strange disconnect seems to stand between, on the one hand, those ethically charged issues that we recognize as threatening to our society and, on the other hand, our professional lives. The 1992 riots in Los Angeles and Atlanta bring vividly to mind the anguish of our cities. Our health-care system is so expensive that it undermines the competitiveness of our industry; at the same time, thirty million Americans are uninsured. Our children lag behind those of other nations in terms of educational performance; and the American family suffers from some combination of economic stress, fractured relationships, and frenetic activity. Perversely, a scientist's conclusion that there is not *yet* a hole in the ozone layer is taken as cause for celebration. And yet, strangely, we allow our professional lives to remain disconnected from these formidable challenges.

Is it that we simply don't understand the significance of

these challenges to us—both as individuals and as business educators and leaders? This seems implausible in a country where our media are regularly faulted for delivering a continuous and negative drumbeat of impending disaster.

It seems, instead, that the disconnect is quite purposeful . . . that as individuals we have lost faith in our leaders and in our institutions, both public and private . . . that we do not wish to commit ourselves to meeting these challenges because to do so—alone and in the absence of trusted leadership—would entail personal sacrifice and the risk of appearing naive, without chance for success. In their book, *The Cynical Americans,* Kanter and Mirvis observe,

Of course, the human condition has always faced some threat to its equilibrium, and the pendulum has always sooner or later, swung back to the point where goodwill and generosity seem to predominate in American society. But these current threats are especially ominous because our political supports have been weakened while the support of the extended family has waned. Moreover, the tendency to behave cynically is being reinforced to an unprecedented degree by a social environment that seems to have abandoned idealism and increasingly celebrates the virtue of being "realistic" in an impersonal, acquisitive, tough-guy world. In citizen and country alike, there seems to be a loss of faith in people and in the very concept of community. Upbeat aspirations for togetherness seem hollow in the selfish 1980s. Cynicism is not a new phenomenon, but today it is especially pronounced.[1] . . . At worst, this negativism produces a self-fulfilling prophecy that foredooms any management message, customer promotion, or proposed improvement. Overall, this corrosive attitude diminishes country and community and, in business, shrinks the fabric of organizational life."[2]

The Leadership, Ethics, and Corporate Responsibility initiative finds its meaning in the very region of this disconnect, among those questions of purpose and principle and responsibility that cynics avoid as too painful, or too risky. Its success depends on our moving beyond negativism . . . on our recognizing not only the inevitable and unhappy future consequences of our current inaction, but also the *immorality* of that inaction . . . on our committing our energies to an attack on these critical challenges to our individual and collective welfare, and to a rebuilding of the trust—in leaders, in organizations, and in one another—and sense of purpose that are so essential to the effective implementation of a strategy aimed at addressing these challenges. Here is where educators can—but do not yet—play their most important role.

There is reason for hope. The very nature of the environmental changes defining management in the 1990s—massive, fundamental, and unprecedented—represents an opportunity; for the force of circumstance renders it nearly impossible to hold on to outmoded educational strategies and structures.[3] They provide ample impetus for broad, sustained discussion of learning objectives and of learning environments, out of which educational change must necessarily come. In such a process, the issues are likely to be reframed as a compelling set of questions—notably different from those on which we have focused in recent decades—and to be managed in a way that invites *all* faculty members into discussions and partnership.

All faculties will ask these critical questions differently. As a point of departure, I would offer the following:

- Who are these twenty-five- to thirty-two-year-olds who come to our schools? How are they "making meaning," and what are their values? What are their assumptions, hopes, and fears? What are their learning and developmental objectives?

- What are the attributes and capabilities that will contribute to effective, ethical, responsible leadership in the decades ahead?

- What is the appropriate balance between the development of attitudes, skills, and capabilities on the one hand, and the transfer of knowledge on the other?

realities of the current learning experience— classroom—from a student's per- ve is the learning experience in the eeded attitudes, skills, and capabili- it in the transfer of knowledge?

blocks of the learning environment er congruence with the learning and es?

g environment and rebalancing our ndamental to the success of the Lead- porate Responsibility initiative. Our e or overshadow what we *are*. The be- ustain our courses and our teaching, uraged and rewarded within our com- are sent (even unknowingly and inad- consistent with the ethics program. tenberg:

s that confirm students in the right- ng cynicism, or that justify their ut the world that lies ahead for them ust be controlled and counteracted. is "let down" by someone on the uni- h time a student feels he or she has ly or arbitrarily, certain weight has egative side of the world's moral bal- re likely that the student will feel freer are less than moral, or to condone the o.[4]

esponsibility that falls upon those of us ster, and staff academic institutions.[5] ues on its chosen road, a number of pro- will undoubtedly be necessary to further strengthen the program, to broaden faculty involvement and support, and to counter the tendency for attention to drift away from the familiar and toward the new. First, there is now considerable interest in introducing a second module at the end of the first year, culminating in a project by diverse teams. In addition to involving additional faculty, such a module would reinforce in the students' minds the seriousness of our commitment and would provide an opportunity to integrate ethics and corporate responsibility into the analysis of a comprehensive case that incorporates lessons from many of the first-year courses.[6] Second, we may emphasize the expansion of electives that attract significant numbers of students from the other professional schools within the university—courses that will help us address the responsibility of business toward the environment, the educational and health care systems, the cities, and other major societal concerns. In addition to connecting future business leaders to the challenges that they must help solve, these courses would allow students from the various schools to explore conflicting ideologies and distorted perceptions that, if left unchecked, might lead to destructive postures of adversarialism. Third, the required capstone course in the second year, Management Policy and Practice, provides an important opportunity to explore questions of individual and corporate responsibility and purpose, to link ethics and principle to leadership and action, and to connect career to a sense of contribution and worth at that vital moment when career choices are being considered. Success in this effort may require a substantial departure from the typical eighty-minute discussion of a case by ninety students, if personal involvement, reflection, and openness are identified as desired outcomes. Fourth, a renewed and visible emphasis on Leadership, Ethics, and Corporate Responsibility will be needed in all of our comprehensive general management programs for executives.[7] The signals sent and encouragement lent to these participants are as important as the messages transmitted to incoming MBA students; for these experienced executives are continuously creating the corporate environments that provide (or fail to provide) the mentoring function on which our young adults depend. On a practical note, these executives give us important insight into the usefulness of various research, frameworks, and pedagogical approaches. And finally, we may develop a formal program on Leadership, Ethics, and Corporate Responsibility for executives, as a way both to test the relevance of these issues and thoughts for practitioners and to broaden and deepen support for the subject within the corporate world.

In some ways these various activities will be no different from all the others now under way. In other words, they must be supported by an extensive, rigorous research and course-development program that is problem centered and management focused, and that reveals principled opportunities for individuals and organizations to contribute to the resolution of the challenges before us. Since the shaping of such initiatives depends fundamentally on the vision and commitment of the faculty directly involved, we must always keep these prerequisites in view.

The most important opportunity, however, is also a major concern; and it is largely outside the control of the business schools. The long-term success of our efforts to integrate Leadership, Ethics, and Corporate Responsibility into the MBA experience will depend on the experience of our graduates as they join and begin their careers in business organizations. Inevitably, these organizations will supplant the professional school. The workplace will serve as the classroom, and managers will serve as real-world teachers. Once again, the signals and messages—intended and unintended—of the joining-up phase will be critical. Recruiters, for example, will convey to prospective managers the reality of the corporate world through the questions they don't ask as well as through the questions they do ask. Hiring and promotion decisions will do much to define which currency really counts within a particular organization—what is valued and what is not. The conclusions drawn from these various experiences, and from the observed actions of senior management, will also feed back into the professional schools. Without question, they will influence the students and faculty whom we hope to engage in thoughtful discussion of Leadership, Ethics, and Corporate Responsibility. It is a closed loop, this world of business and business school; and we can be sure that recent MBA graduates will effectively enlighten those who come after them about what really matters in the corporate world. What is needed, within and across our institutions—public and private, corporate and educational—is a rediscovery of purpose and principle, of responsibility and worth, and of accountability in terms appropriate to the twenty-first century. If companies do not take up this challenge—if they fail to work in partnership with schools to foster a broad and all-embracing approach to Leadership, Ethics, and Corporate Responsibility—then our own unilateral efforts will certainly fail.

The real issue, therefore, is not whether Leadership, Ethics, and Corporate Responsibility can be integrated successfully into our educational programs and our organizations. Experience confirms that we can succeed on both fronts. The real issue is whether our collective will is sufficient in breadth and duration. It may not be. Business schools necessarily reflect the preoccupations and values of their broader social context. They embody (and even distill) the pragmatic, materialistic, restless quality of twentieth-century America. But we must confront the fact that commitment and restlessness are rarely compatible. We must contain the latter if we are to sustain the former. This is only one of our challenges. But it is a challenge that must be met if we are to resolve the pressing, mutually compounding issues that confront American business and American society in the 1990s. It is a challenge worthy of our strongest commitment and our finest intellectual effort.

NOTES

1. Donald L. Kanter and Philip H. Mirvis, *The Cynical Americans* (London and San Francisco: Jossey-Bass, 1989), p. 7.

2. Ibid., p. 2.

3. Commission on Admission to Graduate Management Education, *Leadership for a Changing World: The Future Role of Graduate Management Education* (Los Angeles: The Graduate Management Admission Council, 1990), p. 3.

4. Stephen Joel Trachtenberg, "Presidents Can Establish a Moral Tone on Campus," *Educational Record* (Spring 1989), p. 7.

5. A thorough review of the learning objectives, the learning environment, and the administrative operations is under way at Harvard. Led by Professor James Cash, faculty chair of the MBA Program, the review builds on the research of Sharon Parks (Chapter Two) and involves a broad and diverse set of faculty, staff, and students.

6. The ungraded nature of the module at the outset of the first year has met with mixed reviews. Those who favor it cite the openness of discussion and the absence of competitiveness. Students do not feel that they must have the "right" answer. The absence of grading requirements also is attractive to senior faculty who typically volunteer for this assignment in addition to a normal teaching load. However, some students point to the absence of a grade as evidence of low commitment. Other students, concerned about meeting cumulative academic standards, shortchange the ungraded Decision Making and Ethical Values module in favor of their graded courses. It seems likely that a module offered later in the first year or in the second year would need to be graded. Once the novelty of the MBA experience wears off, it can be assumed that grade pressure in other courses would overwhelm preparation for a nongraded course.

7. Throughout the 1980s, the late Professor John Matthews taught an ethics module in the Advanced Management Program and the Program for Management Development at Harvard Business School. His skill at communicating with executives on issues of Leadership, Ethics, and Corporate Responsibility was of critical importance—not only to these executives, but to the design of the new ethics initiative.

Index